A GUIDE TO XANTHOS
AND LETOON

Sites Inscribed
on the UNESCO World Heritage List

ON THE 50TH
ANNIVERSARY OF THE COMMENCEMENT
OF EXCAVATIONS

INQUANTENAIRE·1951
MISSION ARCHÉOLOGIQUE FRANÇAISE
DE XANTHOS ET DU LÉTOON

Istanbul 2003

The Xanthos team, in front of the former
excavation house (1951)

A GUIDE TO XANTHOS AND LETOON

Sites Inscribed on the UNESCO
World Heritage List

ON THE 50TH ANNIVERSARY
OF THE COMMENCEMENT
OF EXCAVATIONS

Jacques des Courtils

Director of French Archaeological Mission
to Xanthos and Letoon

In Memoriam Pierre Demargne,
the first director of the French Mission.

YAYINLARI

EGE YAYINLARI

Series "Ancient Cities of Anatolia": 4

© 2003 Ege Yayınları & Jacques des Courtils
ISBN 975-807-055-X

Cover picture
Base with bull's head, North Portico, Letoon (Fig. 73)

Translation
İnci Türkoğlu
with the assistance of
John Moorcroft

Graphic Design
Savaş Çekiç

Printing
Graphis Matbaa

Ege Yayınları
Aslan Yatağı Sokak, Sedef Palas Apt. No.35/2 Cihangir
34433 Istanbul - Turkey
Tel: +90 (212) 249 0520 - 244 7521   Fax: +90 (212) 244 3209
e.mail: zero@kablonet.com.tr

Foreword

Visitors to Xanthos feel the strangeness of the monuments they see; when they arrive at Letoon, they feel they have come to a familiar Greek sanctuary. But, wrong! This sanctuary, too, like the city of Xanthos, bears deep traces of the civilizations that brought them into being. Archaeological and historical interest in these two sites grew so much that in 1950 the Foreign Affairs Ministry of France applied to the Republic of Turkey for a license to begin excavations. The digs that started in 1951 still continue under the patronage of the Foreign Affairs Ministry[*]. C.N.R.S.[1] contribute by providing researchers and supplies. The uniqueness of the Lykian (Lycian) civilization and the significance of the finds from excavations culminated in their inclusion in UNESCO's World Heritage List.

The French Archaeological Mission to Xanthos and Letoon has accomplished, under the direction of P. Demargne, P. Devambez, H. Metzger and C. Le Roy, an enormous amount under hard financial conditions. However, after 50 years of work, research on Xanthos is far from over. The Lykian acropolis, the great Byzantine Basilica and Lykian tombs are well known but a greater portion of the city has not yet been explored in detail. Although the excavations at Letoon, which conceals one of the

---

[*] Under the direction of Social, Humanities and Archaeology. AXEL (Friends of Xanthos and Letoon), 2 rue Alponse Daudet, 75104 Paris, has given their support.

[1] IRAM (UMR 5607), Maison de l'Archéologie de Bordeaux III.

best-preserved Greek temples of antiquity, are at a further stage, we are still unable to present a whole picture of the site.

Work completed so far has resulted in numerous publications: monographs, excavation reports and articles[2] but an easily accessible summary of the work has not been available until now. For the 50th anniversary of the commencement of the excavations it was decided, in order to fill in this gap, to organize a public exhibition to present the work done and the current state of both sites, with an exhibition catalogue and an archaeological guidebook. This work, written up by the Director of the French Archaeological Mission, is none other than a collective effort by the previous and present excavation team members and it could not have been realized without their charity and good will. We would like to extend our sincere thanks to D. Louche, Cultural Attaché at the French Embassy, D. Laroche, J.-F. Bernard and L. Cavalier, members of the team, and to P.Y. Saillant (C.N.R.S.) for his contributions and help under various titles.

Jacques des Courtils
Xanthos, August 2001

---

[2] Bibliographical references are given in detail at the end of the book and summarized within the text.

Map of Lykia.

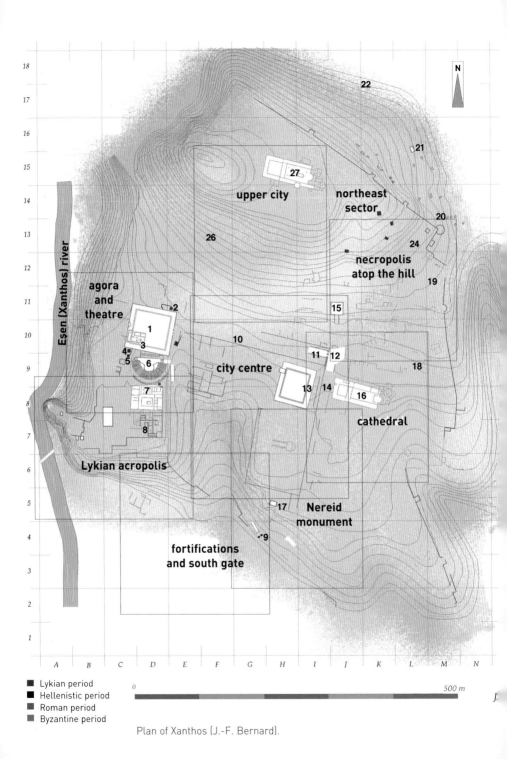

Plan of Xanthos (J.-F. Bernard).

CONTENTS

9

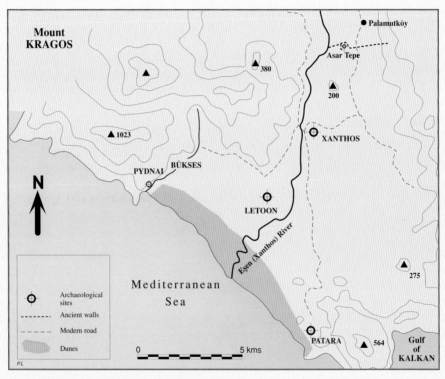

Map of Xanthos and environs.

GEOGRAPHY AND HISTORY OF XANTHOS AND LETOON

Geographical Location

The city of Xanthos is located at the northern end of a triangular plain bordered by the Mediterranean to the south, Pydnai Fort to the west and the city of Patara to the east. Kragos (today's Avdancık/Sandak Dağı) and Antikragos (today's Baba/Boncuk Dağı) mountains soar to the west of this plain, which was formed by alluvium carried by the River Xanthos (Eşen Çayı) from the Taurus Mountains around the end of the prehistoric times. The Massikytos (Akdağ/Alacadağ) mountain range rises to the east. Located on the left bank of the Eşen Çayı, the city of Xanthos was founded slightly above the marshes and swamps that have covered the estuary from antiquity through to recent times. To the north of the Xanthos lies a splendid landscape, evergreen watered by creeks flowing down the Tauruses, in to the valley of Eşen Çayı between the two mountains.

This valley must have been as fertile in the past as it is today and numerous Lykian cities were founded here. Today we can find only a few cedar trees in the mountains covered by pines. However, in antiquity, cedar was dominant. The Lykian cedar mentioned by the ancient writers Theophrastos and Pliny the Elder produced a medium quality timber.

There are a few rocky outcrops in the Xanthos estuary. At the foot of one of them, half way between the city of Xanthos and the Mediterranean –five kilometres from both– is the Sanctuary of Letoon located on a spring now lost due to the rising underground water table.

Though the area is within the Mediterranean region, a cool breeze blows from the nearby Tauruses, which renders the summer heat bearable. Winters meanwhile, are mild on the plain while harsh on the mountains. Thus the locals were semi-nomads and used to move between their villages in the plain and pastures in the mountains according to the seasons. This was certainly how people lived here in antiquity as well.

Chronology

Prehistory	Emergence of the Lukkas, the ancestors of the Lykians.
15th - 13th c	Hittite Empire in central Anatolia. Numerous texts mention the presence of Lukka peoples on the border.
1280 Battle of Kadesh	The Lukkas in the Hittite army fall captive to the Egyptians.
13th c	The Hittite Emperor Tudhaliya IV returns home victorious from his Lykian campaign.
1180 Rukus (Lukkas?)	Of the Sea Peoples invade also Egypt following the east Mediterranean coasts.
12th - 8th c	"Dark Ages" and the "Geometric" Period in Greece. Scarce trace of life in Lykia.
7th c	Potsherds bear witness to the presence of life in Xanthos.

Dynastic Age

546 - 334	The golden age of Xanthos, the biggest town in Lykia, under the Persian rule.
546	Persians conquer Anatolia. The citizens of Xanthos commit mass suicide when the Persian General Harpagos conquers the city. About this time a local dynasty emerges.
Towards 460	Destruction by fire and reconstruction of Xanthos.
Around 460 - 420	The reign of Kuprlli, the Xanthian dynast.
Around 420 - 400	The reign of Gergis
Around 400 - 380	The reign of Arbinas. Construction of the Nereid Monument.
Towards 380	Xanthos first falls into the hands of Perikles of Limyra in east Lykia and then Mausollos of Halikarnassos in Karia.
334	Conquest by Alexander the Great. Alexander passes nearby Xanthos that was integrated entirely into the Greek world.
334 - 166	From Greece to Rome; Xanthos under the control of Hellenistic States.
334 - 300?	Integrated into the Empire of Alexander, Xanthos gains autonomy under the sovereignty of Antigonos.
300 - 197	Xanthos and the Lykian coast are under the sovereignty of Ptolemies, the Hellenic kings of Egypt. The Confederation of the Lykian cities was probably formed in this period and Xanthos was one of the leading members.
197 - 188	Xanthos passes into the hands of Antiochos III the Great, the king of the Seleucids.
188 - 166	Rome hands Xanthos and Lykia over to Rhodes. Numerous riots against the Rhodian representatives.

Lykian Confederation

166 BCE - 43 CE	Golden Age of Lykia, and decline of Xanthos?
166 BCE	Lykians appeal continually to Rome complaining about the Rhodian sovereignty.
166 BCE - 48 CE	Golden Age of the autonomous Lykian Confederation. Letoon Sanctuary of Xanthos becomes the Sanctuary of the Confederation.
44 - 41 BCE	Civil war after the assassination of Julius Caesar. The locals commit mass suicide again when Brutus, one of the murderers, captures Xanthos.
30 - 20 BCE	Augustus forces Xanthians to rebuild their town.
4 BCE	Lucius Caesar, adopted son of Augustus, dies in Limyra.
43 - 395 CE	Romanisation of Xanthos; economic revival.
43 CE	Following civil disorder, Emperor Claudius abolishes the Lykian Confederation and forms the province of Lycia-Pamphylia.
About 45 CE	St. Paul stops at the port of Patara.
138 CE	Emperor Hadrian visits Lykia.
297	Emperor Diocletian founds the tetrarchy and puts forth the first step towards the division of the empire.
330	Emperor Constantine the Great founds Nova Roma, later known as Konstantinopolis (today Istanbul).
395	Upon the death of Emperor Theodosios I, the empire is divided forever and Xanthos becomes part of the East Roman Empire.

Christian Xanthos

5th through 7th c	Last golden age of Xanthos.
5th c	Development of Early Byzantine architecture in Xanthos: Churches and magnificent mansions are built. Xanthos becomes the seat of a bishopric. A church is also built at Letoon.
7th c	Persian (Sassani) raids, followed by Arab fleet epidemics and earthquakes: Xanthos and Letoon are destroyed and abandoned.
8th - 10th c	Hiatus.
8th - 11th c	Bishopric continues to exist despite the demise of the city.
11th - 12th c	Tiny settlement at site. Turcoman tribes move into Lykia. Economic crisis and settling of nomadic way of life.
18th - 19th c	Probably Greeks from Rhodes are settled at site. The village is named after the Kınık tribe of Turcomans.
19th - 20th c	Rediscovery of Xanthos.
1838	Charles Fellows discovers Xanthos during his exploratory trips through Anatolia.
1881, 1882, 1892	Works by Austrian epigraphists.
1950	The Republic of Turkey gives permission to France to excavate at Xanthos.
1962	The Republic of Turkey gives permission to France to excavate at Letoon.

Fig. 1 Lykian landscape. Animals in the Tauruses.

HISTORY OF XANTHOS AND LETOON

Prehistoric Period

Despite the superb geographic conditions of the Xanthian region with its mild climate, well-watered land and fertile soil (Fig. 1), a continuous human settlement in this area during the prehistoric period has not yet been traced. At Xanthos, the digs have reached the virgin soil, however, without finding any trace of prehistoric settlement. A polished stone axe was discovered in the riverbed by chance during the construction of the modern bridge over the River Xanthos (Eşen Çayı) but this is not enough to support any claim for human settlement in the region during the Neolithic period. 20 km north of Xanthos, near Tlos, about forty potsherds contemporary with the Hacılar (6th millennium BCE) have been recovered but so far, the location of their origin has not yet been determined. Therefore, practically nothing is known about the possible prehistoric human life in this region.

Bronze Age

The presence of mankind in the Bronze Age (3rd and 2nd millennia BCE) at the site and the region has not been attested so far. Only in Patara, a bronze axe of Early Bronze Age (3rd mill. BCE) has been recovered, but it has been an isolated find so far. This is quite unusual for this is the time when numerous important sites, such as Troia (Troy) and Alacahöyük, flourished in other parts of Anatolia. Yet, despite the lack of archaeological evidence, the presence of Lykian peoples starting in the 2nd millennium BCE has been traced from evidence from outside the region.

Near Eastern and Hittite texts mention the presence of peoples called Lukka in the western fringe of Anatolia. Though detailed information is not available, it seems that the Lukka peoples and the Hittites had difficult relations. The abovementioned texts tell us that the Lukkas sent warriors outside their homeland: Lukkas were their allies when the Hittites were fighting at Kadesh (Syria) against Ramses II around 1280 BCE (Fig. 2). Similarly, a king of Alasiya (= Cyprus) complains of Lukka raids in a letter to the Egyptian pharaoh Akhenaton. Egyptian texts indicate that the League of "Sea Peoples" including the Lukkas, launched two maritime raids against Egypt (about 1200 BCE).

Finally, a Late Bronze Age an inscription recently recovered in the Yalburt (Pisidia) region shows that the last Hittite king,

Fig. 2   Lukka soldiers held captive by the Egyptians during the Battle of Kadesh (1280) BCE) (low relief from Abu Simbel).

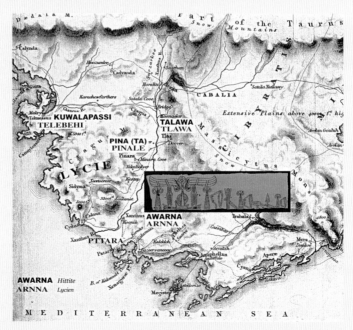

Fig. 3   Map of the Xanthos Valley. The names of the Lykian cities are given in Hittite, Lykian and Greek. The name of Xanthos is given as "Arnna" in the Hittite hieroglyphs of Yalburt Inscription in the window.

Tudhaliya IV, led a campaign there (Fig. 3). According to this text, the following cities existed at that time: Pttar (Patara), Arnna (Lykian name of Xanthos), Tlawa (Tlos), Wanawanda (Oinoanda). Excavations at these sites so far have yielded no evidence for an earlier human settlement in the region.

On examination the language used by the Lykians in the Classical period, it was clearly the language of the Luwian peoples living on the borders of the Hittites. We arrive at the conclusion that peoples, generally called the Lukkas and who were not unified, were living along the western and the southern coasts of Anatolia. It is likely that this name was the origin of the name Lykia used in the 1st millennium BCE. This was the name given to them in the Iliad, composed around 8th century BCE: according to Homer, Lykians were allies of the Trojans and had come from far away lands, from the banks of the purling Xanthos, under the leadership of Sarpedon and Glaukos. The River Xanthos, called the Eşen Çayı today, purls at the skirts of the city of Xanthos. The word "xanthos", meaning "yellow" or "blonde" in Greek, is sometimes translated into the Lykian language, and sometimes both languages mingle with each other.

Thus, we see that the Greeks recognized the presence of the Lykians from a very early period (as of the time of Homer) but gave them a name in Greek. Moreover, the Lykian peoples are not encountered in the same region as in the previous millennium but rather settled in the area where we generally expect them, that is, in the southwest of Anatolia between Fethiye and Antalya.

However, Greek texts other than Homer give different origins for the Lykians... The historian Herodotos (2nd half of the 5th c. BCE), born in Karia neighbouring Lykia, tells that Lykians called themselves "Termilae" in their own language, not "Lykians". Contemporary inscriptions recovered in the excavations bear witness to this claim by Herodotos. Evidently Homer was well informed and tells that the Lykians came from Crete: "A quarrel arising there between the two sons of Europa, Sarpedon and Minos, as to which of them should be king, Minos, whose party prevailed, drove Sarpedon and his followers into banishment. The exiles sailed to Asia, and landed on the Milyan territory. Milyas was the ancient name of the country now inhabited by the Lykians: the Milyae of the present day were, in those times, called Solymi. So long as Sarpedon reigned, his followers kept the name which they brought with them from Crete, and were called Termilae, as the Lykians still are by those who live in their neighbourhood." (Herodotos I, 173).

Such legends are not easy to double-check today but this does not necessarily mean that we should totally disregard them. The text by Herodotos is not entirely untrue: the fact that maritime relations were established between Anatolia and Crete is attested archaeologically by the potsherds of Cretan origin recovered on the southwest coast of Anatolia. However this is outside the area where the Lykians lived! Amongst the pictograms on both faces of the curious Cretan document, the Phaistos disc, the silhouette of a typical Lykian house can be traced (24th sign). In addition, it is possible that the Pelests, in alliance with the Lukkas in the League of the Sea Peoples mentioned above, were of Cretan origin. This handful of clues may be sufficient to consider valid the text by Herodotos...

Consequently, it seems reasonable that the Lykians (or the Termilae) were an Anatolian people of Luwian descent and that they had close relations with Crete. Perhaps they welcomed and intermingled with a people called Termilae migrating from Crete –this migration might have taken place during the raids of the Sea Peoples– but retained some traces of their origins.

Bibliography: E. Laroche, R.A.,1976, 1-15-19; R. Lebrun, Hethitica 1977, 155-158.

Early First Millennium BCE

The Bronze Age came to an end around 1200 BCE for mysterious reasons and the Hellenic, Trojan and Hittite civilizations disappeared suddenly. During this period, mysteriously the raids by the Sea Peoples start again. Then comes an era about which we know practically nothing and thereafter, first in eastern then in the central parts of Anatolia emerge new civilizations, of which Neo-Hittites, Urartians and Phrygians are among the foremost ones. The obscure period in Lykia lasts from 1200 through 700 BCE: we neither have any information about this period nor any records in the historical and archaeological fields. Thus, the recorded history of the Lykian people starts around the year 700. It is worth noting that even this date is based on very poor evidence: a few potsherds of this period recovered at Xanthos and Letoon form the earliest evidence for the settlement at the site (Fig. 4). For the first half of the 6th century, the Xanthian acropolis presents remains of structures and potsherds of Anatolian origin as well as of ceramics imported from mainland Greece.

Bibliography : H. Metzger, FdeX, II.

Fig. 4 Potsherds of Archaic Period recently recovered at Xanthos.

Archaic and Classical Periods

The Lykians take their place on the stage of history by mid-6th century BCE. About this time the Persian king Kyros sends his general Harpagos over to Anatolia in order to conquer the whole area. After capturing the Lydian Kingdom and its capital Sardis, Harpagos proceeds south: he captures Karia and reaches the Xanthos plain probably in 546 BCE: "When Harpagos, after these successes, led his forces into the Xanthian plain, the Lykians of Xanthos went out to meet him in the field: though but a small band against a numerous host, they engaged in battle, and performed many glorious exploits. Overpowered at last, and forced within their walls, they collected into the citadel their wives and children, all their treasures, and their slaves; and having so done, fired the building, and burnt it to the ground. After this, they bound themselves together by dreadful oaths, and sallying forth against the enemy, died sword in hand, not one escaping." (Herodotos I, 176).

From then on Lykia was under Persian rule until Alexander the Great liberated it in 334 BCE. However, with Alexander, it passed directly to Hellenic sovereignty. Xanthos was ruled by a dynasty, who we do not know whether was local or of Persian origin, for the most part of this period from the end of Archaic Period (around 500 BCE) through the Classical Period (500 through 323 when Alexander the Great died) (Fig. 5). This dynasty known as the Harpagids might be the family of the general Harpagos who captured Xanthos in 546. We do not have enough evidence to reconstruct the historical frame: anonymous tombs, coins bearing the names of the rulers but nothing else and a few texts half recovered and hard to interpret are the evidence available.

Lykians seem to have been loyal subjects to the Persian king during the two centuries under the yoke. A Lykian leader named Gergis, son of Ariazos, fought in the Persian army at the Second Mede War in 482 when the Persians occupied the mainland Greece. It is also known that a fleet of 50 Lykian ships under the command of Kyberniskos, son of Sikas, was sent to join the Battle of Salamis. This information provided by Herodotos may, of course, include some errors of transcription and we suggest that the names given by him should be corrected as Gergis, son of Harpagos and Kybernis, son of Kossika. In both cases these names belong to Xanthian rulers of the end of this era.

Bibliography: O. Treuber, Geshichte der Lykier, 1887; T.R. Bryce, The Lycians, I, 1986; A. G. Keen, Dynastic Lycia, Brill, 1998.

Potentates of the 5ᵗʰ Century

There is almost no information available about the 5ᵗʰ century history of Xanthos. The only concrete information at hand is that a single dynasty ruled continuously. We know the name of some of them: Kuprlli ruled between 480 and 440, after him Keriga and Gergis came. No details are known regarding their reigns. We know the first potentate only from the coins bearing his name; and the second and the third ones are known from the Xanthian inscriptions mentioning them. The history of this dynasty is probably told in the great Lykian inscription on the Inscribed Pillar (2); however, we are not able to decipher this text at present.

In this century, Lykia changed sides at times: From the Greek sources we learn that they joined the Athenian (Delian) League and stayed until, maybe until after, 440. However, the fact that an Athenian general called Melesandros died struggling to bring Lykia back to the League shows that in 429 BCE Lykia was already back on the Persian side.

Gergis (around 420 - 400?) is known to have been open to Greek culture: though he boasts that he killed with his own hands seven Greek soldiers (hoplites from Arcadia) he had several verses in Greek inscribed on his tomb and arranged for his successor, Arbinas, to receive his education from a Hellene teacher.

Bibliography: O. Treuber, Geschichte der Lykier, 1887; O. Morkholm – J. Zahle, ActaArch, 43, 1972, s. 57-113; O. Morkholm – J. Zahle, ActaArch, 47, 1976, s. 47-90, J. Bousquet, FdeX, IX; A. G. Keen, Dynastic Lycia, Brill, 1998.

Fig. 5   Lion relief from Xanthos (6ᵗʰ centruy BCE).

LYKIAN DYNASTIC COINAGE

The Lykians started to mint money about the end of the 6th century BCE when their country was entirely under Persian rule. The coinage was silver and interestingly enough, Lykian towns used two different standards: western Lykia, including Xanthos, preferred the widespread, current Greek standard (called attico-euboic) while eastern Lykia minted in the Persian standard, which was heavier.

The coinage bears various symbols. At the beginning, the reverse side had the "carré incus", the simple, hollow mark made by the engraver's point, more or less square in shape. However, in a short period of time both faces of the coins started to be decorated with figures: heads of gods in the Greek style (e.g. Zeus, Apollon, Artemis, Athena), real animals (e.g. boar, lion) or imaginary animals (e.g. winged horse, sphinx). A curious sign with three legs, called "trisceles", whose meaning is not clear, is also seen. The presence of the Greek deities and their depiction style point to a strong Greek influence, imitating the Greek coins.

The location of the mint is given in the inscriptions; unfortunately however, these are only abbreviations denoting either Lykian towns (Tlos, Telmessos...) or the rulers, whom we generally do not know from any other source, such as Kuprlli, who reigned in Xanthos in the 5th century BCE. The abundance, variety and quality make the Lykian dynastic coinage a remarkable example of its time but analysis is very difficult for we do not know the reason for this wealth: the protection of the Persian king, the commercial prosperity of Lykia, or something else...

This magnificent coinage of the dynastic period disappeared about 360 BCE for reasons unknown. No more minting is seen until 166 BCE when the Lykian Confederation liberated itself from Rhodian rule. As of this date a common coinage bearing the phrase "Lykian people" came into use. This federal monetary system continued until 43 CE when Lykia became a Roman province.

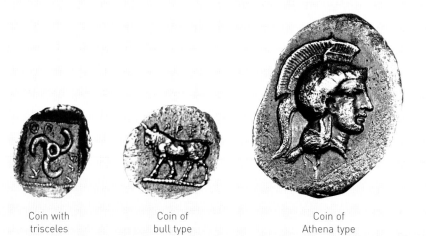

Coin with   Coin of   Coin of
trisceles   bull type   Athena type

Arbinas

Arbinas, who ruled at the beginning of the 4th century, was probably the last potentate of this dynasty but also the most brilliant and the most devoted to the Hellenes. We understand that he had a hard time ascending the throne but managed to hold on to it, and to keep Tlos, Pinara and Telmessos (today Fethiye) under his sovereignty and rule them just as his predecessors had. Thus, a Xanthian king ruled the greatest part of the Xanthos valley.

Arbinas was brought up by a Hellene nanny. Then he stayed with Symmachos of Pellana, who was a Hellene sage and he would also consult the oracle at Delphoi at times. During his reign the number of Greek texts in the Lykian inscriptions doubled (Fig. 6). Finally he had a magnificent tomb built for himself: The Nereid Monument (17), an imitation of a Greek temple. All these indicate the dominance of Hellenic culture and this cultural expansion was certainly supported by the potentate himself. In religion too Arbinas had an important role for he altered greatly the cults at the Letoon Sanctuary.

Following Arbinas, who died about 380 BCE, Xanthos lost its primacy: the cities in the Xanthos valley first fell into the hands of Perikles of Limyra in east Lykia, then to the rulers of Halikarnassos in Karia, namely Pixodaros, younger brother of the famous king Mausollos. The trilingual inscription of Letoon calls him the "satrap of Lykia".

Bibliography: J. Bousquet, FdeX, IX; D. Asheri, Fra Ellenismo e Iranismo, Bologne, 1983.

Fig. 6   The Lykian side of the bilingual inscription from Letoon, honouring Arbinas.

Hellenistic Era

With the conquest of the whole of Anatolia in 334 BCE by Alexander the Great, Lykia, too, became part of the Hellenic civilisation (beginning of the Hellenistic Era). As of this date Greek influence started to increase: The Lykian language disappeared from inscriptions and was replaced by ancient Greek; and in architecture Greek styles were adopted. Lykia became a province of the Greek world.

During the Hellenistic Era, Lykia was tossed between various dynasties following Alexander the Great: for a short time Lykia was captured by the Seleucids of Antiocheia (today Antakya in Turkey) and then during the 3rd century was under the rule of the Hellenic Ptolemies of Alexandria, Egypt; at the beginning of 2nd century once again passed into the hands of the Seleucids for a short while and then was awarded to Rhodes for their support of the Romans at the battle against the Seleucid king Antiochos III (Fig. 7).

The period under the Rhodian rule (188 - 166 BCE) was a dark spot in history. Lykia seems to have had internal problems throughout but details are scarce. The Lykians sent representatives to Rome twice and complained about the conduct of the Rhodians. When the Rhodians lost the friendship of Rome, they had to leave Lykia in 166. The following brilliant period lasting until 43 CE is known as the Lykian League (or the Lykian Confederation).

The Lykian League has a special place in the history of antiquity as an independent state (but one which came under Roman sovereignty in time) and had a very modern structure.

Fig. 7 Inscription honouring Antiochos III the Great from Xanthos (early 2nd century BCE).

This league was under the direction of a leader called the *Lykiarch*, whose power was controlled by an assembly of city delegates. Each city participated in the assembly with a number of delegates in proportion to their population: big cities like Xanthos had three, medium sized cities had two and small ones had only one delegate to represent them.

The foundation date of the Lykian League is not known: though it is usually given as 166 BCE with the departure of the Rhodians, various evidence suggests that it had commenced even earlier. In both cases the only valid point is the fact that the Lykians were grateful to the Romans for liberating them from the yoke of the Rhodians; therefore, they organised a festival of

Xanthos at the end of antiquity, virtual view from the north (J.-Cl. Golvin). The Mediterranean fortifications and the grand squares of the Roman period particularly stand out. In the background: the mediterranean is flanked by the slopes of Patara on the left. The fortress of Pydnai is the right. The sanctuary of Letoon is partly concealed behind a rocky hillock.

Romaia-Letoia. Naming their chief goddess after goddess Rome and deifying the Roman State they identified Leto with Rome. The theatre at Letoon must have been built in order to facilitate this festival. Following this, they continuously presented a cult to the goddess Rome, or deified emperors or imperial family members.

Bibliography: O. Treuber, Geschichte der Lykier, 1887.

Roman Period

The Roman period was not perfectly peaceful either. During the war that broke out after the assassination of Julius Caesar by his adopted son, Brutus, in 42 BCE, Xanthos was invaded by the murderer and his men. Historian Prokopios tells that just as 500 years before when the Persians besieged the city, the Xanthians again committed mass suicide when Brutus laid siege; however, there is not enough evidence to support this claim. Yet, the city must have gone through a terrible period for it is seen in a letter from this period that emperor Augustus orders the Xanthians to rebuild their city!

Apart from this period the Roman era progressed in wealth and peace, as verified by numerous monuments and luxurious buildings. Nevertheless the city is not mentioned very much. It was definitely under Roman rule just as the rest of Lykia and it was joined with neighbouring Pamphylia to form the province of Lycia-Pamphylia. In the reign of Nerva (end of 1st century CE) Xanthos gained the title of "the metropolis of Lykian people" and a privileged position; however, this title did not go beyond a symbolic meaning for the other Lykian cities of Tlos, Patara, Telmessos and Myra are also mentioned with the same title.

An earthquake shook the town around 145 CE and the theatre was subsequently rebuilt with the personal financing of Opramoas of Rhodiapolis, a wealthy Lykian citizen. Despite a healing of the wounds and extensive construction works carried out, it is seen that Xanthos lost in importance compared to other Lykian cities. For instance, Myra and neighbouring Patara with its excellent protected harbour stepped to the for.

Bibliography: O. Treuber, Geschichte der Lykier, 1887; A. Balland, FdeX, VII.

Byzantine Era and the End of Xanthos

Xanthos was christianised in the early Byzantine era (5th and 6th centuries) and became the see of a diocese as most other Lykian cities, but we lack data about this period in the history of the site. Apparently the city retained its wealth; luxurious mansions and grand churches were built in the course of the 5th century. In spite of plague in 542, this brilliant period lasted well into the 6th century but came to a tragic end: Persians invading Rhodes attacked Lykia as well. Having attained a great naval victory at sea off Phoenix in 655 Arab forces established permanent control of this part of the Mediterranean. The destruction by two earthquakes one after another a few decades apart added to the destruction by the Arabs. The Xanthians hastily restored the fortifications not in use since the Roman times (Fig. 8). At the end of the 7th century the city was abandoned gradually into solitude for a few centuries.

Xanthos was reconstructed on a modest scale twice. It was re-inhabited in the 11th century but this time the churches were of a much more modest size. This reconstruction lasted only a short

Fig. 8 Fortifications of Xanthos built in the 7th century reusing blocks from Roman edifices.

century. With the defeat of the Byzantine army at Malazgirt (Manzikert) in 1071, and especially after that at Myriokephalon in 1176, Turks started to arrive in Anatolia. Nomadic Turkish tribes settled in the region. Some of them were from the Kınık tribe, hence the name of the modern village. About this time there might have been a settlement, feeble though, amongst the ruins of antiquity and Byzantine era, but a great fire in 13th century initiated a long silence.

The last settlement at the site started in the modern era, in the 18th century, probably by Greek villagers who rebelled in Rhodes and therefore were re-settled by the Ottoman Sultan. A few ruins from this settlement, remains of houses, stonewalls with no mortar, have been located in recent years. These houses were built with stones from ancient ruins and mainly used as stables. When Charles Fellows arrived at Xanthos in 1838 he met a handful of Greek villagers. With the last citizens abandoning the site and establishment of the Kınık village at foot of the hill excavations began.

Bibliography: C. Foss, "The Lycian Coast in the Byzantine Age", Dumbarton Oaks Papers 48 (1994), s. 1-52.

LYKIAN LANGUAGE

The Lykian language is known from dozens of inscriptions on stones dated to 500 - 300 BCE (Fig. 9). These texts recovered at Xanthos, Letoon and other Lykian sites can easily be transliterated for the Lykian alphabet is a derivative of the Greek alphabet. The Lykians added only half a dozen more signs and adapted it to their own language. A few bilingual inscriptions – that is, in ancient Greek and Lykian languages – helped start the deciphering of the language; however, these bilingual texts are usually very short – only the trilingual inscription of Letoon is longer, see p. 145-146 – not providing all the keys to the grammar. Yet, linguists generally are of the opinion that Lykian language is an Anatolian (Indo-European) language and that it is related to the Luwian

Fig. 9   Lykian language (The Inscribed Pillar, no. 2).

language that was a relative of the Hittite language spoken in central Anatolia during the previous millennium. Deciphering of the Lykian language is still in progress today but there still are gaps and incomprehensible sections. With the progress of excavations and other developments a longer bilingual text, that will play the role of the Rosetta Stone, maybe discovered and only then will it be possible to solve the mysteries.

REDISCOVERY OF XANTHOS AND LETOON

An Englishman, Charles Fellows, going on an extensive exploration tour around Anatolia in 1838, rediscovered Xanthos. Influenced by it very much he returned to the site in 1840 and stayed for a while. He returned again in 1842 and 1844 for longer stays. During his last two visits he was able to carry out some digs and carry away numerous sculpture and architectural blocks for which he had official letters of permission. After a short while his finds were put on exhibit in three halls at British Museum. However, though Letoon was also discovered at the same time, it did not attract attention for excavations.

In 1881 and 1882 Austrian scholars, the epigraphist Benndorf and the architect Niemann, visited Xanthos and compiled ancient inscriptions.

Finally in 1950 the French Archaeological Mission under the direction of P. Demargne obtained official permission from the Republic of Turkey to carry out excavations at Xanthos and started working in 1951. The same team then commenced work at Letoon in 1962 first under the direction of H. Metzger and then C. Le Roy. The excavations at Letoon have advanced further and research work has started on the reconstruction of the Temple of Leto. The present team focuses on restoration at Letoon and excavations at Xanthos.

Bibliography: Ch. Fellows, Asia Minor. A Journal written during an Excursion in Asia Minor 1840 (1841); Ch. Fellows, An account of Discoveries in Lycia, being a Journal kept during a second Excursion in Asia Minor (1841); E. Slatter, Xanthus, Travels of Discovery in Turkey, Londra 1994; H. Metzger, Dossier de l'Archeologie, 239, December, 1998.

A VISIT TO XANTHOS

It is possible to see the city centre of Xanthos and the temples at Letoon in an hour for each site. Going from one site to the other, a 5 km secondary road, should take 15 minutes. Visitors with more time or interested in details should spare 3 hours for a thorough visit to Xanthos and 2 hours for Letoon.

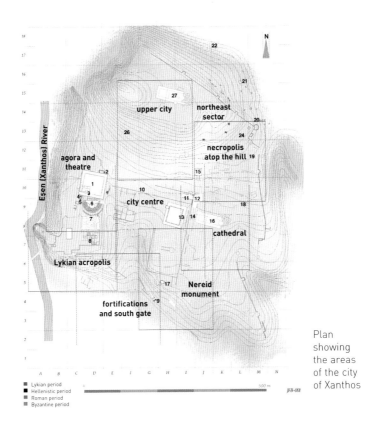

Plan showing the areas of the city of Xanthos

THE SITE OF XANTHOS

The city of Xanthos is located on the left bank of the River Xanthos (today Eşen Çayı). The site covers a wide hill called the "Roman Acropolis" or the "Upper Acropolis" though it does not give the impression of an acropolis in the historical sense. To the south of this main hill lie three ridges, the southwest of which is the Lykian Acropolis falling in a gorge down to the River Xanthos flowing 60 meters below, hence deserving its name, being the best fortified part of the city at all times (Fig. 10).

For a quick tour, it may be sufficient to stay around the Lykian Acropolis. For a long tour, the Lykian Acropolis is visited first starting from the Agora; then the Bishopric Basilica is visited on the inner part of the site; and finally one needs to head towards the North Necropolis, climb up the hill and descend down to the Agora, a splendid view of the site.

Fig. 10   Lykian Acropolis, view from south. Xanthos (Eşen) River in foreground.

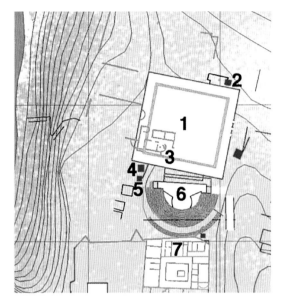

Agora and theatre.

AGORA AND THEATRE

Roman Agora (1)

Next to the road and situated at the centre of the site this square contains a cluster of important monuments and is flanked with pillar tombs and the theatre. Today the Agora appears as a large square surrounded by colonnaded porticoes of Roman times. Crossing the parking lot to the west, one enters the Agora through a triple monumental gate whose threshold is still *in situ* (Fig. 11). Just to the north of this gate are scattered remains of a pool of a fountain built for strollers to refresh themselves. A little further is an interesting monument inscribed on all sides:

Fig. 11 View from north of the Agora and the Theatre. Lykian Acropolis in the background.

The Inscribed Pillar (2). Further south, by the modern road is the first Lykian monumental tomb.

This house-type tomb (Fig.s 12 and 13) stands on a stepped foundation concealing a low room hewn partially from the bedrock; above is the tomb imitating a timber structure (note the timbers on the lid). It is usual for the Lykian tombs to be multi-storeyed. Inscriptions on other tombs indicate that each was meant for a family. Such tombs have their upper chamber spared for the leading member of the family while the lower chamber was meant for the other members of the family. This example before us probably dates to the 5th century BCE.

Fig. 12   East portico of the Agora and the house-type tomb.

Fig. 13   Drawing of the house-type tomb (Scharf).

47

From the porticoes encircling the Agora square only the three-stepped krepis has survived. The krepis used to support the columns in front and the foundations of the back wall. A few column bases can still be seen *in situ* on both sides of the gate and in the east section of the north portico. The columns which stood on these bases have not survived to this day but a few columns of blue veined marble lie around. No capitals for these column shafts, which could have belonged to the porticoes, have been recovered. However, numerous fragments belonging to the entablature have been discovered in their second use at the agora at a later time. These fragments comprise smooth frieze blocks of the architrave and smooth cyma cornice blocks ornamented with lions' heads, which were only decorative and did not function as rain gutters, as was usual with this type of decoration. The floors of these porticoes were paved with plain white mosaic with coarse tesserae, traces of which can be seen here and there.

The two inscriptions recovered near the gate do not provide enough information to determine their purpose. One bears the name of the Roman emperor Nerva while the other one has become illegible in time. Yet, from the legible parts we learn that between 81 and 84 CE the governor of Lycia province, C. Caristanius Fronto, had built a bouleuterion, the location of which has not yet been discovered. We do not know for certain the date of the construction of the Agora. The ornamentation of the porticoes indicates the Flavian Period (mid or latter half of the 1st century CE).

At a later time the Agora square was occupied by a church and its cemetery (6th - 7th century), then abandoned, and reused in the 11th and 12th centuries and abandoned again for good until today. You may notice traces of reuse in the northeast corner of the Agora, where rough walls built with rubble block the passages between portico elements. These details betray two phases: first a less modest replica of the portico, then the intercolumnar openings were filled with a continuous wall, perhaps concealing houses behind.

Later around the 18th century, Xanthos was resettled, perhaps by Rhodian villagers resettled here by the Sultan. These villagers might have kept their animals here in the Agora. Traces of lighter structures enclosed with walls of reused ancient material and bumps may be evidence for use as stalls.

Bibliography: J. des Courtils – M. Boënnec, AnatAnt, VI, 1998, 459-461.

Inscribed Pillar (2)

The monument closest to the gate of Agora is known as the "Inscribed Pillar" or the "Obelisk of Xanthos". The inscriptions on the pillar form, in a sense, the historical archive of ancient Lykia but this information cannot be reached for the present because the deciphering of ancient Lykian language has not been fully accomplished. This monument stands on a piece of stone shaped from the bedrock (Fig. 14). Its foundation has two levels: the lower tier of the foundation was built with multiple blocks whereas the block on top is monolithic. This base of 1.26m height has horizontal dimensions of 2.50 x 2.60m and on top, we can see remains of big tenons, typical of Classical Lykian architecture. On top of all rose the pillar, fragments of which have been recovered; so the original height was 4.04m.

This pillar was a tomb characteristic of Lykia, and in Xanthos, of the six monuments that have survived five are still standing (Fig. 15). The Inscribed Pillar was surmounted with a burial chamber, fragments of which found their way to the British Museum and Istanbul Archaeological Museum. The monument was built with slabs of local ordinary limestone, was of 1.54m height and was decorated in relief with scenes of battle: marching soldiers, a wounded soldier falling on his head, a victorious commander proudly walking across the battlefield. These reliefs certainly depict the heroic deeds of the person buried in the chamber. Fragments of the enormous lid that was decorated with projections along the edges and that must have once covered this chamber lie around. This lid once supported a throne, whose armrests were decorated with lions' heads. The total height of the monument reached 9.71 m! There must have been a statue of a seated figure on top of it but not one fragment has been recovered so far.

Inscriptions (Fig.s 9 and 14), still visible, on all sides certainly tell the heroic deeds of the person whose statue surmounted the monument. The fact that the Lykian language has not yet been fully deciphered stops us from understanding everything in detail; however, on the north face is a short inscription in Greek which reads:

"Since the sea separated Europe from Asia, nobody amongst the Lykians has been able to erect on the wall of the Agora a monument depicting their victories and similar to the stele of the Twelve Gods.

Here, Gergis, son of Harpagos, defeated, with the strength of his arms, all the young Lykians of his time, captured many

Fig. 14   The Inscribed Pillar, view from south. The burial chamber has not survived.

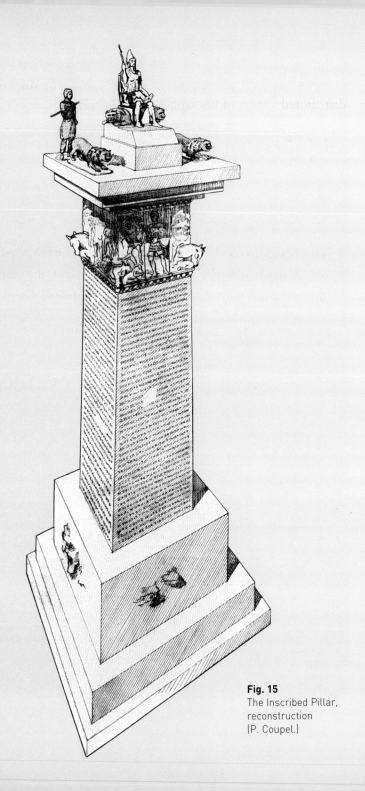

Fig. 15
The Inscribed Pillar,
reconstruction
(P. Coupel.)

acropolises with the help of Athena, besieger of the cities, and distributed shares of his kingdom to his relations.

After all this, the Immortals gave him the award he deserved. He, in the same day, killed seven *hoplites* from Arcadia. He, only he amongst all the mortals, erected many monuments of victory in the name of Zeus, and crowned the tribe of Karikas with brilliant deeds." (translated by J. Bousquet)

This text tells us the identity of the owner of the tomb. Gergis died around 400 BCE, so we have an idea of the date of the monument. According to this text, Gergis defeated Greek soldiers (*hoplites* from Arcadia); therefore, the depiction of a soldier defeating another must represent him, and moreover, the six shields represent the others. Furthermore the text in the Lykian language mentions a Milasandra, who is believed to be Melesandros of Athens. The historian Thucydides tells Melesandros was a general from Athens who was killed in Lykia during a campaign (429 BCE).

All this provides us with a wealth of information. The fact that Melesandros is mentioned helps us to date the reign of his Lykian enemy to the end of the 5th century. This date also confirms the style of the reliefs, a bit mediocre but surely of the Classical Period. It is a little paradoxical to rely on a short text in ancient Greek after a long text in ancient Lykian language, yet it proves that he lived in a period when the Lykians were in contact with the culture of their enemies.

Finally, we learn that the tomb is dedicated to the gods and was built within the *temenos* of an Agora. This gives us the most valuable information about city planning in the Lykian period. According to the text, the square where the monument was built must be an agora of the Classical period; therefore, we believe that the agora continued to exist in the Roman period even though its function in Roman times has not yet been determined. However, apart from the inscription mentioning an agora, there are no traces of the first Agora. Recent research and soundings at various points showed that the Roman porticoes were directly built on levelled bedrock; in this case the Roman architects must have cleared all traces of earlier periods.

Finally, new information yielded by decipherment studies shows that the Lykian inscription also mentions the tomb of Arbinas, son and successor of Gergis; therefore, the text was inscribed on the Pillar Tomb after the deaths of both potentates, that is, long (ca. 20 years) after the erection of the monument itself.

Bibliography: P. Demargne, FdeX, I; J. Bousquet, FdeX, IX, 155-99.

Religious Complex in Southwest Corner of the Agora (3)

Towards the end of the 6th century a small church of the Early Byzantine Era was built in the southwest corner of the Agora. The floor of the church was paved with mosaics, almost all of which have disappeared. In the apse, remains of a *synthronon* and an ancient column drum reused as an altar leg can still be seen. To the north is a small chapel and a room whose floor paved with mosaics is under protection today. It is thought that the entire building was destroyed in the 7th century. About 60 tombs of the same date were unearthed in this area. The tombs yielded a few very poor, bronze, and even iron, accessories and goods. The fact that some tombs were dug into walls already destroyed and levelled off indicate that these tombs were made after the destruction of the building.

Just to the west of the agora lies a wide unexplored area. Here are traces of a large building with porticoes of Corinthian capitals and dating to the Severans (?). This structure, which might have been a civilian basilica, could have been converted into a church with the addition of a semicircular apse extending into the western portico of the Agora.

Bibliography: A.-M. Manière-Lévêque, AnatAnt, VI, 1998, 463-468; VII, 1999, 372-374; VIII, 341-366.

Harpy Tomb (4)

To the southwest of the Agora, diagonally opposite the Inscribed Pillar, stand two more pillar tombs. The larger of the two is also older and is known as "Harpy" or "Harpies Tomb"

(Fig. 16). The original reliefs in white marble decorating the burial chamber are in London and depict fantastic creatures, half-woman half-bird, and therefore, have been identified with the Harpies of Greek mythology. The total height is 8.60 metres while the height of the monolithic block forming the pillar measures 5.43 metres (1.5 metres taller than the Inscribed Pillar) by 2.30 metres wide. The base measures 4 metres long by 3.80 metres wide by 1.40 metres tall. The lid-stone is also enormous with dimensions of 3.80 metres x 3.5 metres x 0.44 metre. There is an opening for maintenance purposes on the west side of the burial chamber (Fig. 17). The small dimensions and height from the ground of this small opening suggest that the dead were cremated and the ashes were put in an urn together with gifts and placed into the chamber through this opening.

What the decoration in low-relief depicts is not known clearly. On the middle slabs of the panel are a scene with alternate figures – male and female – seated on a throne and other figures simply standing in respect or presenting arms. The most interesting detail is at the extreme ends: fantastic creatures with female heads carry an infant. These creatures have been identified as Harpies, the mythological creatures who carried the souls of the neonates dying unexpectedly.

These reliefs are certainly in the Greek (Hellenic) style. Given that no other monument of early date at Xanthos is of marble it is possible that its artist was a Hellene from Ionia because its very "enveloped" style is similar to the Milesian finds. The postures of the figures are like those seen in the late Archaic period of Greek sculpture; especially the women standing on the west side, who are quite similar to the reliefs depicting the "Passage of Theoros

Fig. 16 Harpy Tomb as seen from the agora.

Fig. 17 Hary Tomb, west side. The opening provided access into the burial chamber.

to Thasos" or the "kore" statues. Though the artist made use of numerous elements (presentation of arms) borrowed from Greek art we are not able to make a general analysis (what is the role of the Harpies?).

This monument, dated around 480 BCE from the style of the reliefs, is the last resting place of a Lykian king whose name has not come down to us.

Bibliography: P. Demargne, FdeX, I, 1958.

Pillar Tomb with Sarcophagus (5)

A few meters to the south of the Harpy Tomb stands another pillar tomb (Fig. 18). This is the only example of its kind: instead of having a burial chamber on top of a monolithic pillar, here is a sarcophagus resting on a base built with blocks. The sarcophagus imitates timber architecture, just as the house-type tomb we saw by the modern road. This tomb is dated to the 4th century BCE from a few motifs in the Greek style. Yet its owner is unknown and its dating is not certain as we shall see below.

The sarcophagus itself was of course found empty but the excavators were surprised when they found an undisturbed burial in the base that escaped the looters. The few pieces of jewellery and a vase of Egyptian faience recovered are on display at Antalya Museum today. On the vase there is a depiction of the queen Berenice, wife of Ptolemy II (283 -246 BCE). With all the data taken into consideration, this burial can be dated to the 3rd century BCE, when the Ptolemies ruled the entire south coast of Anatolia. Pottery fragments within another burial encountered under this 3rd century burial helped clarify the historical sequence as follows: the monument was built in the second half of the 6th century; the sarcophagus was added in the 4th century; it was reused in the 3rd century.

Other tombs seen around these two monumental ones are simple pits dug into the rocky ground. Also found were traces of a square building with a burial chamber in the centre. It is thought that this area was used as a necropolis (cemetery) until the 3rd century BCE. Recently, another tomb of the same period was also unearthed a bit to the north under the church in the southwest corner of the Agora. Thus, we understand that the

Fig. 18 Pillar Tomb with Sarcophagus. The sarcophagus imitating local timber architecture rests on a pillar formed by huge slabs.

Lykians continued to bury their dead within the city even during a time of extreme Hellenization, while the Greeks buried their dead outside the city.

Bibliography: P. Demargne, FdeX, I, 1958.

Theatre (6)

The theatre of Xanthos (Fig.s 11 and 19) is located in a natural valley separating the Acropolis from the rest of the city. The traces of the first theatre built here can be seen in the orchestra section. This construction in the shape of a stone circle is the only trace from the first orchestra. Traces of a stage building independent from the rows of seats *(koilon)* have also been found. The first structure dates to the Hellenistic Era.

The construction of the theatre made inevitable the displacement of a Lykian tomb. This monument can still be seen semi-buried under the upper rows of seats in the east. This monument, called the Pillar Tomb of the Theatre, is of particular interest: the

Fig. 19 The Roman theatre of Xanthos. Auditorium as seen from the Byzantine fortifications. The agora in the background is seen.

workmanship of the chevrons with excellent polishing covering all the four sides of the monolithic pillar is particularly fine. The Greek inscription on the pillar was completed when the missing parts were recovered and we know that the structure had to be re-placed in antiquity. The name of the architect who managed this hard job is Onasandros, son of Onasandros.

The theatre structure we see today is from the 2nd century CE and is a single structure with its rows of seats and the stage building, typical of Roman theatres. First there were about 20 rows divided into 11 *kerkides* (cuneiform divisions) by stairs and the uppermost row had seats with high backs forming sort of a balustrade for the *diazoma* (the walking way). In antiquity the first five or six rows from the bottom were dismantled and a wall with a masonry of mediocre quality was built, which was meant obviously to protect the spectators when the theatre was used for wild beast fights.

The upper tier of the theatre originally rose much higher than today but only four rows of this tier have survived; the others were dismantled during the Persian and Arab raids in the 7th century CE and were re-employed in the construction of the fortifications above the theatre. Pieces from the theatre can still be spotted in the wall. The upper tier originally standing on vaulted substructures was divided into 22 *kerkides* by stairs. In the east, traces of the *vomitorium*, the vaulted corridor entranceway for spectators, can still be seen. The theatre was not large; its capacity is estimated to be around 2200 people.

As was usual in Roman theatres, the rows of seats used to lie over both entranceways *(parodoi)* and joined the stage building; however, there is an unusual feature: the eastern *parodos* opens

The Harpy Monument and the Pillar Tomb with Sarcophagus on top. In the foreground, the rows of seats of the theatre bear the traces of a violent earthquake.

into the street stretching from the City Gate to the Agora while the western was a fake one, not opening anywhere for it was built into the bedrock only to provide symmetry. The stage building consisted of a raised platform, on which the actors performed, backed with a colonnaded two-storey façade, whose blocks are scattered today. At the back were rooms for cloakroom and storage. All the structure fell down in an earthquake whose magnitude the badly disturbed western seats betray.

The date of the first Roman restoration of the theatre is not known. An inscription mentions that an important Lykian patron, Opramoas of Rhodiapolis, donated 10,000 *denarii* for the reconstruction work after the earthquake of 149 CE. This is certainly for the repair of an already existing structure. However, the style of the architectural decoration suggests a date around the end of the 2nd century. Perhaps, the work financed by Opramoas was for the repair of the Hellenistic theatre and after a while, some parts of the structure were destroyed somehow and alterations had to be carried out.

Bibliography: E. Frézouls, CRAI, 199, 875-890.

LYKIAN ACROPOLIS

When we pass the theatre to the east going south, we reach a gate in the Early Byzantine fortifications. These walls, quite similar to those at Ankara built in the reign of Konstans II (641 - 668), were most likely built during the Arab raids in the 7th century in order to shrink the size of defences and to fortify this part of the city. Remains of earlier walls, of probably 5th century BCE, with the same defensive purpose have been uncovered under these walls in the east. In the Byzantine Era, this area was refortified towards both the city centre and outside the city.

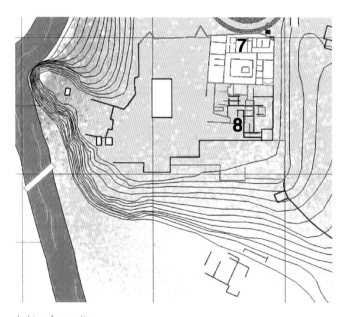

Lykian Acropolis.

Instead of entering directly into the Lykian Acropolis, if one follows the *diazoma* towards east, one can examine the pillar tomb, which was relocated in antiquity, and the fortifications in this part. The east face of these fortifications built in the 5th century BCE presents a beautiful example of polygonal masonry (Fig. 20). This masonry technique, in which the Lykians excelled themselves, is thought to belong to the Greeks. However, the Lykians had been using this polygonal masonry, long before the Greeks, from the 6th century BCE through Roman imperial times at Xanthos and other parts of Lykia.

Fig. 20 Eastern fortifications on the Lykian Acropolis, with polygonal masonry (5th century BCE).

The interior of the acropolis presents a paradoxical layout: here the walls of 6th century BCE houses lie under the walls of a magnificent mansion of the Early Byzantine Era (5th and 6th centuries CE). For the construction of the Early Byzantine mansion the land was levelled, destroying the traces of Hellenistic and Roman structures; however, the Lykian structures buried much deeper survived.

From the gate one emerges into a road. This road used to lie to the south and was flanked with luxurious mansions on both sides.

Early Byzantine Mansion (7)

Upon entering the Lykian Acropolis the visitor sees the well-preserved Early Byzantine Mansion on the left (Fig.s 21 and 22). Covering an area about 2000 square-meters this mansion consisted of rooms surrounding a central courtyard (Fig. 22, no.4). The courtyard was originally paved with terra cotta plates concealing a cistern (no.3) cut into the bedrock and covered with a brick vault. On the east side is a three-niched fountain (no.2) built with brick and faced originally with marble. There are porticoes on the other three sides forming a peristyle. The columns supported a roof sheltering the corridors behind, which were paved with polychrome mosaics with geometric designs. All the rooms opening into these three corridors were probably paved with rich mosaics as well. In the northwest is an interesting section opening into an inner court (no.5) with a well in it. A small water canal in the mosaic pavement of the big room kept the room humid all the time (no.7).

Fig. 21 Early Byzantine mansion, view from the southwest.

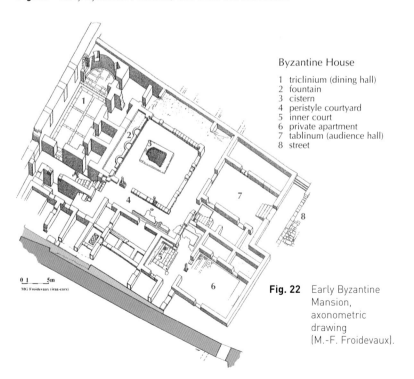

Byzantine House

1 triclinium (dining hall)
2 fountain
3 cistern
4 peristyle courtyard
5 inner court
6 private apartment
7 tablinum (audience hall)
8 street

Fig. 22 Early Byzantine Mansion, axonometric drawing (M.-F. Froidevaux).

The stairs in the northeast corner of the peristyle courtyard follow the natural slope down to the lower floor. Under the stairs there are the remains of two pools revetted with marble and their water came via conduits from upstairs. This vestibule room was also accessible from outside via a doorway which was later blocked. It is likely that this entranceway was kept for guests of honour because this room gave access to a grand hall decorated luxuriously (Fig. 22, no.1) (Fig. 23). Oriented north-south the grand hall *(triclinium)* ends in the south with an elevated apse covered with a semi dome.

The floor of the grand hall was paved with black (schist) and white (marble). There were no columns supporting the super-structure; the column pieces seen here have fallen down from the peristyle courtyard above. The walls were originally plastered and painted, of which no trace has survived. This hall certainly was a *triclinium*, i.e. dining hall, or a reception hall for guests. Small rooms adjoining on the west were probably for service purposes and their lateral walls were plastered ending uniformly 50 cm before the rear walls. It is thought that these rooms housed big cupboards.

Returning to the road crossing the acropolis in north-south and continuing southwards, we see another Early Byzantine mansion in ruins. The mosaics uncovered here are on display in Antalya Museum. However, before reaching that, the large cistern cut into the rock on the right hand side might be from the Lykian period. To its west are the remains of a wall built with finely worked large ashlars probably of a temple from 5th or 4th century BCE. On the east the cistern borders the road. Roughly opposite the temple are the remains of another structure, which

Fig. 23 Early Byzantine Mansion, triclinium, view from the north.

are thought be the foundations of the so-called "temple with three cellas". However, there are more interesting remains on the southeast and southwest of the Lykian acropolis.

Bibliography: H. Metzger, FdeX, II, 19; H. Metzger, FdeX, IV, 1972; A.-M. Manière-Lévêque, AnatAnt., VII, 1999, 375-379; VIII, 2000, 341-346; IX, 2001, 231-237.

Lykian Houses (8)

To the southeast of the Acropolis there are walls standing to a height of some 3 meters and built with rubble and mud mortar (Fig. 24), a primitive technique that dates back to very old times, the first half of the 5th century BCE. In fact some walls are even earlier. The structures comprise rectangular rooms adjoining each other but lacking doorways and windows. In the course of excavations, a thick layer of ash designating a great fire was encountered. Thus, it became clear that the conserved walls belong to the foundations of elevated timber houses accessible via stairs from outside only. The stonewalls of the ground floor

Fig. 24   "Houses" on the Lykian Acropolis (5th century BCE). These walls supported a timber upper storey.

encircled storage rooms and could only be reached via the rooms upstairs.

Such structures have been unearthed only on the Lykian Acropolis of Xanthos. Neither in the rest of the city, nor in other parts of Lykia have similar structures been found. Their large dimensions suggest that they were built as residences for the rulers of Xanthos. Next to them are remains of storage halls, which can be easily repaired and used again. These comprise rectangular rooms whose long walls are furnished with a sort of bench for huge baked clay storage jars *(pithoi)*. Such structures for storage are also found in the palaces of the Near East, Crete and Hittite Empire. These finds prove the existence of a centralised economy that was administered from the palace. Since we know that this system was abandoned in the first millennium BCE, we should question whether or not it was still in effect at Xanthos at this time.

This type of construction with a ground floor of stone walls (sometimes replaced with brick) and a timber upper floor was also used by other ancient Anatolian peoples. Especially in the 2nd millennium BCE it was employed by the Hittites as witnessed at Hattusha and Maşat Höyük. The great interest in this type of construction by the Lykians can be verified by the abundance of forests in their country. The Lykian tombs present a striking example of this: the rock tombs have been sculpted as if built with timber. It is even possible to think that the pillar tombs, characteristic of Lykian culture, were meant to recall the elevated (hanging) houses we saw in the Acropolis. In Üzümlü, 30 km north of Xanthos there is a modern building whose ground floor does not have any openings and the upper floor has been arranged as a terrace. This structure resembles one of the houses in the Acropolis rather than a pillar tomb.

Bibliography: H. Metzger, FdeX II.

Western Buttress

The Lykian Acropolis rises above the River Xanthos, flowing to the west some 60 meters below. Leaving the Acropolis one passes by Monument G, dated around 460 BCE, from which nothing remains other than the foundation integrated into the southern fortifications of the Acropolis. Numerous fragments with sculpted decoration belonging to this monument were recovered in the early years of the excavations (Fig. 25). Monument G seems to have been a stone structure standing on a high platform and imitating timber architecture and was decorated with statues (Fig. 26). Its exact nature is not known but it is thought to be the Tomb of Sarpedon who was the legendary ancestor of the Lykians and had a cult. We learn from texts by Appianos that the "Sarpedonion" was still standing in the Roman times and that numerous fragments were well preserved.

The platform built with finely worked ashlars on the western extreme of the Acropolis is the foundation of a Lykian structure, named Monument F. From the pieces recovered we can see that Monument F, just like Monument G, imitated timber construction. Pottery and jewellery finds recovered nearby suggest that it was used as a cult centre from the times it was built (around 460 BCE?) through Hellenistic times.

Fig. 25 Relief of horsemen from Monument G. (ca. 460 BCE).

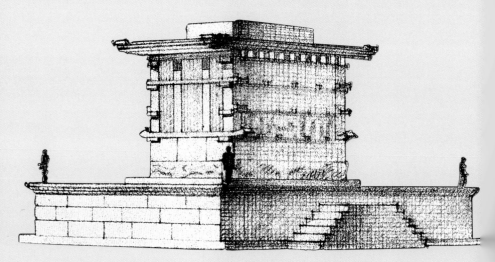

Fig. 26 Lykian Acropolis, Monument G (reconstruction by P. Coupel).

FORTIFICATIONS AND SOUTH GATE

The Xanthian fortifications have a perimeter of about 2 kilometres. The city walls of Xanthos are preserved here and there in parts, having been abandoned and reconstructed throughout history. Leaving Kınık village, arriving at Xanthos, visitors pass by the South Gate on the fortifications, which can also be reached walking down the asphalt road from the parking lot towards the village.

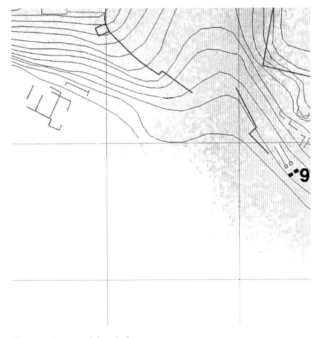

Fortifications and South Gate.

South Gate (9)

The South Gate of Xanthos has a bayonet-layout, quite popular in antiquity. Soldiers normally held their shields with their left arms, so attackers trying to penetrate into the city had their right side unprotected, vulnerable to the soldiers on guard.

The South Gate was built in two distinct phases. From the first phase, the right gatepost has survived partially and the left one is more intact. The right gatepost is buried for the most part under the modern road while the left one is a real bastion with its height over 5 meters (Fig. 27). South Gate is a beautiful example of Lykian architecture of the Classical Period. It was built with extraordinary workmanship shown in the excellent fitting large polygonal stones and ashlar facing. The extremely voluminous corner blocks fit superbly between courses and assure the cohesion of the whole. We do not have any idea at all regarding the superstructure of the gate. The sculpted cornice blocks, lying in the entryway today, were brought down here from various Roman structures in higher parts of the city and used to narrow the passageways for security purposes probably during Arab raids in the 7th century.

The inscription on the right gatepost, legible today, is dated to the reign of Antiochos III (beginning of the 2nd century BCE) and states that this Hellenistic king dedicated the city of Xanthos to the deities Leto, Apollo and Artemis. These leading deities of Xanthos were honoured at Letoon Sanctuary. The inscription also mentions the allegiance of the city to the king; therefore, it is possible that the inscription was effaced on purpose when the city regained its independence in 166 BCE. Another inscription in

Fig. 27 South Gate, left bastion (polygonal masonry, 4th century BCE).

which the citizens thanked the same king has recently been recovered.

On the backside of the first gate there is an arch, still standing today, rising from a Doric entablature (Fig. 28). The metopes of the frieze of the entablature are decorated with busts of Leto, Artemis and Apollo in low relief. An inscription on the architrave, still legible today, states that the arch was erected between 68 and 70 CE in honour of the emperor Vespasianus by Sextus Marcus Priscus, the Roman governor of Lycia.

Fig. 28 South Gate, Arch of Vespasianus, erected by the governor S. Marcus Priscus (68-70 CE). This arch embellished the south entranceway to the city.

On the South Gate, the "Apollonic Triad" (Leto, Artemis and Apollo) appear twice: first, in the inscription of Antiochos III and then as reliefs on the Vespasianus Arch. This is not surprising because, as far as we know today, the road entering the city through this gate came from the Letoon Sanctuary.

A few hundred meters to the west of South Gate, the remains of a Roman bridge are still visible under the modern bridge over the Eşen Çayı (River Xanthos) today. To see the remains, one needs to go over the modern bridge and pass the Roman baths. The road passing over the bridge led south, to Letoon. The exact route of the road cannot yet be determined but a significant Roman *necropolis* a few hundred meters south of the bridge gives an idea of its route; for in antiquity the dead were buried along the road leaving town (for ease of access). This *necropolis* is outside the village of Karaköy and can be reached via the road along the right bank of Eşen Çayı past the village towards south. Numerous sarcophagi were found here in the last century but today none are *in situ*; today only the scant remains of a *heroon* are visible. This detour is recommended only to visitors with a deep passion for antiquities.

Bibliography: J. des Courtils, Nouvelles données sur le rempart de Xanthos, REA 96 (1994), 285-298.

CITY CENTRE

Recent excavations (2000) carried out in this part of the city have revealed a group of edifices dated to the Roman period – paved streets, squares and porticoes. These structures were built during a re-planning of the city whose date is unknown. This may have been a general rebuilding, repair work after an earthquake, or a planned enlargement of the town centre.

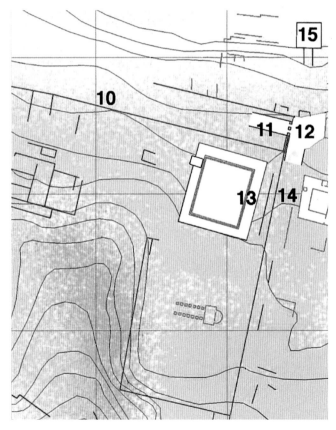

City centre.

Colonnaded Street (Decumanus) (10) and Upper Agora

Leaving the parking lot to the east the visitor first sees the remains of a street among the bushes. Excavations yielded a well-preserved street paved with large white limestone slabs under the present level. This main street crossing the town east to west is the equivalent of the east-west street called "decumanus" in Roman cities. The roadway itself was 11.85m wide between two sidewalks, which were paved with mosaics and sheltered under porticoes. A main street flanked with roofed porticoes on both sides was typical of antiquity. This layout emerged in the East during the Hellenistic Era and was taken up by Roman architects for their monumental appearance. We can see the same layout in other towns of Lykia, such as Phaselis and Kadyanda but the one at Xanthos is much more sumptuous. Behind both porticoes lay a series of shops; the northern ones leaned against the ascending slope of the hill above the whole area.

Excavations since 2000 have brought to light a large square (Upper Agora) to the south of the Decumanus. Covering an area of approximately 2500 square-meters, this square was flanked on all four sides with colonnaded porticoes paved with polychrome mosaics. Various column fragments and bases show that the porticoes were built in the Corinthian order. The floor of the square was paved with fine limestone slabs. The use of this square is not clear for the present.

Bibliography: J. Des Courtils – L. Manoukian-Cavalier – C. Quichaud, AnatAnt VIII, 367-371; VIII, 339; IX, 227-231.

Dipylon (11)

Recent excavations (1998 - 2000) have unearthed, at the end of the colonnaded street a monumental gate of a rare type, a Dipylon, from the Early Roman Imperial period (Fig. 29). Triumphal arches generally have three vaulted passageways– not two. However, here a massive central pier built with roughly worked voluminous stones is flanked with two smaller piers on both sides. The lateral piers stand at the intersection of the porticoes. The coffers on *intrados* of the vaults were decorated with animal figures, plants and motifs like "Herakles' knot" in relief. This triumphal arch, with all its grandeur, indicates that one arrives at a paved junction, which is flanked partially by

Fig. 29   Dipylon, view from the east (before reconstruction). This arch marked the entrance to a paved square.

structures of a later date. The base of an honorary statue of an important citizen of Xanthos, Publius Claudius Telemachus, who lived at the end of the 2nd century CE, was reemployed in the construction of the monument.

Other stones with inscriptions belonging to this triumphal arch were also recovered: For instance, a cornice plate is dedicated to four demi-gods, or deified tetrarchs. Another plate bears the names of emperors Valens and Valentinianus (around 375 CE). It is thought that the monument was built probably in the latter half of the 4th century and stood until a late date when it was destroyed in an earthquake. The area was cleared and arranged in the course of the 2000 excavations.

Bibliography: J. Des Courtils – L. Manoukian-Cavalier – C. Quichaud, AnatAnt VIII, 367-371; VIII, 339; IX, 227-231.

Paved Square (12)

The colonnaded east-west street *(decumanus)* intersects at the Paved Square with another one descending from north to south *(Cardo)* (Fig. 30). An important example of Roman urbanism at Xanthos is observed here: apart from the triumphal arch we have just mentioned, this paved square is flanked with a grand incurving monument (under examination) on the north and a *cryptoporticus* on the south; the excavations have not yet shed light on the contemporary structures on the east side, where a structure of a later date stands today. Meticulous exploration will show that these different urban planning activities are not perfectly in accordance with each other: though the *Cardo* and the *Decumanus* intersect at a right angle, the *cryptoporticus* and the incurving monument to the north are not aligned with them.

Fig. 30 City centre, view from north. Centre: remains of the Dipylon.
Right: Decumanus. Left: the Paved Square and the Cardo.
Background: Cryptoporticus.

Moreover, the angle between the two different pavements of the
square conforms to the alignment of the two latter monuments.
Thus, it can be inferred that this paved square was located at the
junction of two different parts of the city with two different
angles of orientation. The finds, such as statues of emperors and
inscriptions of decrees honouring politicians, coming from recent
excavations around the square, suggest that the structures
surrounding it must be of official character.

*Bibliography: J. Des Courtils – L. Manoukian-Cavalier –
C. Quichaud, AnatAnt VIII, 367-371; VIII, 339; IX, 227-231.*

Cryptoporticus or Civil Basilica (13)

An important building is located to the southwest of the intersection point of the two main streets, and its façade extends as far as the beginning of the *Cardo*. This structure (Fig. 31) built at the same time as the porticoes of the Upper Agora mentioned above, was designed on two storeys making use of the slope of the terrain. The upper floor is at the same level as the porticoes of the Upper Agora and the east-west street while the ground floor opens to the north-south street lying at a lower level.

Fig. 31
Civil Basilica.
Ground floor, east side,
before the
excavations.

There was a line of shops facing the north-south street, and behind the shops was a big cistern within the foundation of the structure. The cistern comprised a long north-south tunnel and was originally roofed with a vault of rubble stones bound with cement; it lined the entire length of the building and was divided into various chambers by walls. It was the main water tank of Xanthos and replaced a larger cistern fed by a much older water system under the rear wall of the same structure. Today traces of the mouth of the older cistern roofed with a domical vault of fine worked ashlars are still visible. This first cistern was probably built in the late Hellenistic Era (2nd or 1st century BCE). There are underground cisterns of similar construction in other cities of Lykia, such as Kadyanda and Termessos. Such structures are usually built under wide, empty areas to avoid the load of structures above. The presence of an earlier cistern and a later cistern replacing it when the Roman structure was built show us that the first cistern was located under a square at the beginning, which was later rearranged and framed with porticoes in Roman times.

At the same time the porticoes surrounded the upper floor of the structure, a three aisled basilica with a 7m wide central aisle flanked with a much narrower side aisle on both sides. The side aisle on the west is at the same time the corridor of the east portico, while the other side aisle on the east is also the portico facing the north-south street *Cardo*. Separated from each other by columns, the three aisles on the upper floor communicated with each other.

The south wall of the rectangular hall on the north opened into all three aisles of the basilica via three arches. The fact that numerous inscriptions of official character from the Roman period were recovered in this rectangular hall suggests that it was the civil basilica. The façade facing the north-south street was bordered with a preserved parapet on which a series of columns crowned with an entablature of alternating horizontal and curved architraves formed a sort of loggia. This type of façade was characteristic of the 2nd century CE. Besides, an inscription dedicated to Emperor Hadrianus was recovered within the structure, which also supports this dating.

Examining the foundations of the *cryptoporticus* and noting the reused material brought from other structures we can see that the south section of the structure had to be rebuilt to a great extent following an earthquake.

Bibliography: J. Des Courtils – L. Manoukian-Cavalier – C. Quichaud, AnatAnt VIII, 367-371; VIII, 339; IX, 227-231.

Structures to the North of the Paved Square

A large building lined the north side of the Paved Square (12). The existence of such a structure came to be known only in 1999 and excavations have not commenced yet. According to observations, the structure located at the north extension of the north-south street *(Cardo)*, was shaped like a half moon. The façade curves inward while at both ends it was decorated with a projecting architrave carried by granite columns. At the foot of the gradient, on the edge of the Paved Square, two *torsos* belonging to emperor statues of the 2nd century CE have been unearthed (Fig. 32). The structure is thought to be a monumental fountain *(nymphaeum)* but we have to wait for the results of excavations to be certain.

There are the remains of a monument (15) on the terrace behind the so-called fountain structure, above the Paved Square (12); this is thought to be of high importance. The structure not only stood above the junction of the two main streets but could also be seen from far away. The foundation, which has survived, has polygonal masonry of big stones at the corners and regular courses along the sides. This technique blending different types of masonry was usual in Lykia. The structure, which is square in plan, opens to the landscape on the south through a corridor *(dromos)* or a staircase. From this mixed construction technique it is thought to date back to the Classical Era, probably to the 4th century BCE, but there is no information at hand about the edifice itself. As no other foundation is visible inside, it is thought that it was filled with earth. It is out of the question to have a massive and important edifice on top and the most likely possibility is a small Lykian structure imitating timber ones. The spolia of stone used in the great Basilica (16) of Early Christian Period (4th and 5th centuries) further down might have been taken from such a structure, probably from here.

Bibliography: J. Des Courtils – L. Manoukian-Cavalier – C. Quichaud, AnatAnt VIII, 367-371; VIII, 339; IX, 227-231.

Fig. 32 Cuirass Torso of an emperor (2nd century CE). This statue was found on the Paved Square and certainly belongs to one of the monuments near the Dipylon or the Fountain.

CATHEDRAL or EAST BASILICA (16)

The East Basilica of Xanthos lies on the east side of the north-south street (Fig.s 33a and 33b). It is likely that this was the cathedral of the Byzantine times. This church is 74m long together with its atrium and has very rich decoration. The edifice built in the 5th century underwent alterations several times.

One enters first the atrium, almost square in plan, paved with terra cotta and surrounded with porticoes on all four sides. The stylobate, walls and columns of this courtyard were built mainly with spolia gathered from earlier structures, particularly Lykian monuments. The floors of the porticoes were paved with poly-chrome geometric mosaics (Fig. 34). We were able to identify that two different artisan groups worked here and that they were both influenced heavily by the style, called "rainbow style", which emerged in Syria towards the end of the 4th century, and influenced the entire East Mediterranean for a century and a half. This style is marked by interlocking motifs, compositions with different centres, chromatic search (rainbow) and the fractioning of the motifs into very colourful small elements.

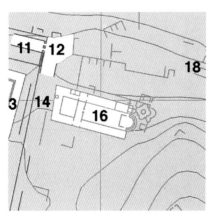

Cathedral.

The eastern portico of the atrium also formed the narthex of the basilica and was separa-ted from the lateral porticoes by double-arched doorways. The narthex communicated with the main hall via five doors, three of which open into the nave. The middle one, still standing today, was built with huge blocks taken from a

Roman gate, probably belonging to a temple now lost. It was flanked with a doorway on both sides again with similar construction. At both ends, a small doorway opened into the side aisles. The floor of the narthex was paved with very interesting mosaics. There are beautiful panels in front of the two lateral doorways opening into the nave: one is filled with stylised floral motifs while the other has a better quality of craftsmanship both in colours and lines. The latter panel has a depiction of garden landscapes beyond fences, as if seen from each side of a square kiosk but applied side by side on the same plane– perhaps it referred to the Garden of Eden. In front of the doorway opening into the northern aisle there is another panel with two deer drinking water from a crater of life in the centre and encircled with floral motifs and bird figures.

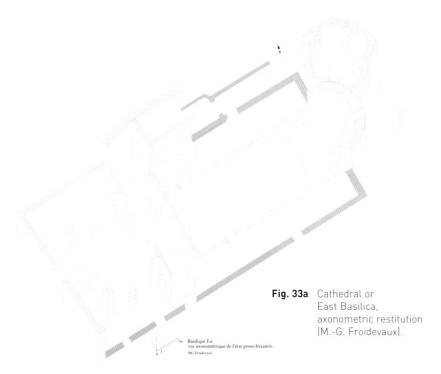

Basilique Est
vue axonométrique de l'état proto-byzantin
MG Froidevaux

Fig. 33a Cathedral or East Basilica, axonometric restitution (M.-G. Froidevaux).

Fig. 33b   Cathedral, view from the west: the atrium in foreground, apse in background.

The floor of the church itself is paved with mosaic, just like the floor of the atrium, but not of the same origin. The excavations tell us the nave was first paved in the *opus sectile* technique; however, after a short while, at the end of the 5th or the beginning of the 6th century, probably due to an earthquake, the nave and the south aisle collapsed destroying the *opus sectile* and mosaic pavements. Fragments recovered from the mortar of the nave mosaic helped reconstruct the geometric compositions of the *opus sectile* pavement. The columns separating the nave from the side aisles were of white or coloured marble and rose on bases. Perhaps there was a gallery floor.

The mosaics of the nave and side aisles are in a worse state than those of the atrium. Besides being destroyed with the collapse of the building, they were also further broken up when

Fig. 34 Mosaic pavement from the Cathedral.

the area was used as a cemetery. The nave mosaic was mostly composed of geometric motifs while there are a few vases and an interlocking arched cross in the centre.

The apse walls, better preserved, are noteworthy for the spolia, typical of Lykian architecture, used in their construction. There was an altar, the traces of whose four legs are still visible in front of the *synthronon* at the foot of the apse wall. Excavations uncovered a curious arrangement at these four legs: four separate water canals came to an end here. This unique arrangement is unexplained for the time being, but it should be related to the peculiarities of the local Christian cult. Traces of the chancel screen before the choir can still be seen but only a few fragments of the marble and limestone screen have survived.

The north aisle adjoins a section that may be called a baptistery. This unusual edifice is quatrefoil shaped and has a baptismal pool in its floor (Fig. 35). This pool, whose steps were faced in marble, was divided into two with some sort of wall. Four pipes filled the pool with water. The entire baptistery was decorated very richly: the opus sectile pavement of the floor is still in very good condition, but the marble facing on the walls and the mosaics of the vault have not survived.

The basilica shared the same fate as the city and was abandoned in the 7th century following an earthquake even worse than the first one. Later, between the 11th and 13th centuries it was partially reoccupied after repairs. The north portico of the atrium was divided into chambers and decorated with frescoes that have survived partially and are under protection today. The

Fig. 35 Cathedral, Baptistery, baptismal pool recovered with its original marble revetment.

baptistery was redesigned and a chamber decorated with frescoes and covered with a vault was added (Fig. 36); the baptismal pool was filled in and the eastern apse of the quatrefoil edifice was altered with the construction of a synthronon. This small but well finished church took the place of the 5th century basilica. This state of the church provides us with very clear idea about the situation of the city during this period. A big fire in the 13th century destroyed the entire edifice.

Bibliography: J.-P. Sodini, Une iconostase byzantine à Xanthos, Actes du colloque sur la Lycie antique, 1980, 119-148; J.-P. Sodini – M.-P. Raynaud, AnatAnt., VI, 1998, 469-471; J.-P. Sodini – M.-G. Froidevaux – M.-P. Raynaud, AnatAnt., VII, 1999, 380-388; VIII, 366-374; IX, 237-241.

Fig. 36 Cathedral, fresco fragment from the reconstruction phase of 12th century (Excavation house depot).

NEREID MONUMENT (17)

Following the ancient *Cardo* (14) further south, one reaches a large square flanked with porticoes on all four sides and its colonnades, the Lower Agora, which is on a lower terrace than the Upper Agora. Unfortunately little remains from this recently unearthed square. In particular, no fragments of the entablatures of the porticoes, each piece of whose architrave must be 4.80m long, have survived. The remains seen here belong to a Christian Basilica that has not yet been excavated.

Let us continue our way further south. When we arrive at a terrace lower than the Lower Agora, sitting above the South Gate (The Arch of Vespasianus) we see a double foundation that

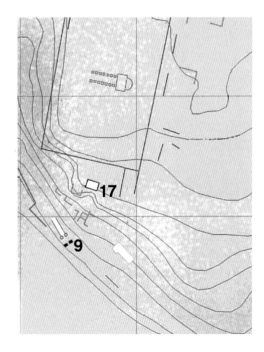

Nereid Monument.

Nereid Monument (beginning of the 4th century BCE) reconstructed at the British Museum (London).

belongs to one of the most beautiful monuments of the Classical Era, the Nereid Monument (Fig. 37). This monument was discovered by Charles Fellows in 1840 and was transported to London almost in its entirety and soon perfectly reconstructed. At the site today only the foundation and a few blocks lying there since very early excavations are visible.

The monument was erected at the edge of a terrace sitting above the city gate. As we will see, the location of the monument is related symbolically to the person who had it built.

The partially preserved foundation was built with local limestone in a technique peculiar to Lykia (joggle and mortise stone plate). It supported a small Ionic temple built entirely in white marble, including its roof tiles and framework. Deep mortises and metal T clamps indicate that this monument was built by Greek, perhaps Athenian, artisans. The stone benches lining the inner sides of the *cella* walls may have been benches to sit on for the funeral banquet.

The sculptures were of exceptional richness and quality: the foundation was capped with two friezes in low relief and was surmounted with a decorative moulding. The sculpture in the frieze surmounting the cella walls was the same as that of the architrave, which is very unusual for Ionic architecture. The decoration had hunting and combat scenes along with a scene depicting a man in Persian costumes, sheltered under an umbrella held by a servant, addressing the people. As inferred from here, the whole iconography bore royal and Orientalising features at the same time.

Fig. 37 The Nereid Monument was probably built as a mausoleum for King Arbinas.
This edifice bears characteristics of Lykian and Greek architecture and art.
(drawing by J.-F. Bernard)

The nature of the subject represented and the sculptural and architectural style suggest a date around 380 BCE. There is no inscription providing the name of the deceased, but it is possible the building was the tomb of the potentate Arbinas who ruled around the beginning of the 4th century BCE. As a matter of fact, the character of the tomb fits perfectly this personage bearing both Persian and Greek identities and the Ionic columns here are similar to those at the Erechteion in Athens: Arbinas was under the rule of the Persian king but, as many inscriptions bear witness, he was brought up in the Greek culture.

The name of the monument comes from the fabulous statues of female figures with the feet of sea creatures standing between the columns. These figures were the Nereids, the daughters of the sea, who accompanied the souls of the deceased, so the name fits the monument perfectly. However, J. Bousquet recently proposed that the monument should be called the Elyana Monument. Elyanas were the goddesses of the springs of Lykia and were honoured at Letoon. Arbinas had made great contributions to Letoon.

Bibliography: P. Demargne, FdeX, III; W.A.P. Childs – P. Demargne, FdeX, VIII; J. Bousquet, FdeX, IX.

NORTHEAST SECTOR OF THE CITY

This sector covers the east flank and lower skirts of the hill above the entire site. Though it is away from the large squares and the backbone of the city – the east-west main street – it was important in antiquity. The other important gate of the city, the North(east) Gate, is in this sector. Besides, the best examples of Lykian type tombs are also found here. I recommended you follow the route suggested below.

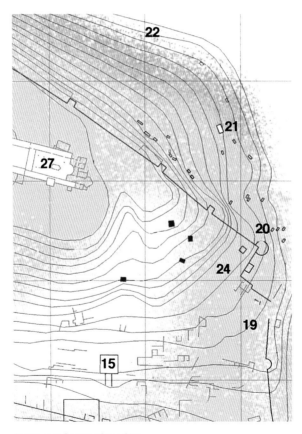

Northeast Sector of the City.

Sarcophagus of the Dancers (18)

Leaving the Paved Square at the junction of the east-west main street and north-south main street and following the path to the north east winding through bushes one reaches the Northeast Sector of the city, which is full of many interesting monuments. About 200m to the east is a Lykian sarcophagus standing on a terrace over the plain. It is known as the "Sarcophagus of the Dancers" after the women figures on its lid (Fig. 38). It was damaged by plunderers but has recently been restored by archaeologists to its original appearance.

This excellent white limestone sarcophagus has the usual arrangement in tiers of the Lykian tombs: a foundation, a monolithic pillar, the chest of the sarcophagus and ogival lid. The craftsmanship on the surface of the stone blocks is particularly admirable. The monument is dated to mid 4th century BCE from the style of the decoration on the lid.

On the long sides of the lid there are four protuberances to allow it to be lifted. These were sculpted in the form of lions' heads but have been weathered by the centuries. The figures can be observed better around midday when the sun illuminates both sides.

On the west side there is a depiction of a boar hunt (Fig. 39). Two hunters –the one on the right riding a horse, the one on the left on foot– attack the boar. Both hunters are dressed with large tunics fluttering in the wind. On the other side is a combat scene: one of two horsemen is falling down defeated from his horse. The victor is depicted wearing armour and standing on the protuberance, he holds his shield as a sign of victory.

Fig. 38 Sarcophagus of the Dancers, south end. (4th century BCE).

103

Fig. 39   Sarcophagus of the Dancers, decoration on the west side of the lid: boar hunt.

The short sides of the sarcophagus can be observed best during early or late hours of daylight and are decorated with fine women figures placed in frames imitating timber structures. These "dancers" wear elegant *chitons* fluttering with their movements. Their presence here should not be related with a joyful moment. These figures must belong to dance rituals of religion, probably of funerals, widespread in antiquity.

The owner of the sarcophagus is not known. There is no inscription at hand. It is likely that he was a wealthy Xanthian and had his personal tomb decorated with hunting and combat scenes, popular among aristocrats.

Bibliography: P. Demargne, FdeX, V.

Lion Tomb (19)

Continuing along the same path we come to a mild slope on the north side of the north fortifications, partially covered with vegetation. There were important constructions here in the Early Byzantine Era. For instance, it is easy to see that blocks from older structures were reused in the fortifications constructed hastily during Arab raids in the 7th century.

A little further, the remains of the oldest pillar tomb of Xanthos, unearthed long ago, can be seen in a ditch. When Charles Fellows discovered it in 1840, he named it the "Lion Tomb" for the slabs forming the burial chamber and on display at the British Museum today are actually decorated with lion figures. We date it to the second half of the 6th century BCE from the influence of the Archaic Greek art observed in its style. This work is one of the oldest examples showing how Greek art influenced Lykian art. The lion motif was widespread both in Hellenic and Middle Eastern regions. For the Greeks, the lion was a guard of the tomb, symbolising death, whereas the oriental peoples connected the figure, as Persian and Assyrian lions show, with the ideology of absolute power. At the time when this monument was erected, Lykia was under the rule of Achaemenid Persians and Xanthos was ruled by a local dynasty subordinate to the Persian king. Perhaps the Lion Tomb belonged to one of the early members of this dynasty and being a subject of the Great King, he chose this symbolic animal of his king.

Bibliography: P. Demargne, FdeX, I.

North Gate of the City and the Northeast Necropolis (20)

Following the path, one passes through fortifications in poor condition. Then turning left towards the Northeast Necropolis one will see on the left the North(east) Gate hidden under vegetation (Fig. 40). This gate, one of the two city gates known for the time being from the stone blocks lying around, had collapsed. The gateposts, which are still standing, are two enormous monoliths, finely worked examples of Lykian architecture. Amongst the blocks scattered around are some rectangular ones imitating tree trunks; so the superstructure of the gate was of Lykian type. Again among the scattered blocks are some voussoir blocks, probably of Roman date. Thus, we can see that the gate underwent repairs and alterations in the course of time; however, excavations have to be carried out for definite information about the North Gate.

The wall makes a right turn to the north on the left side of the gate and continues, a beautiful wall with regular masonry, which is unusual for Lykian architecture. The wall ends at a large round tower and again making a right turn continues towards west, up the hill. The tower at the corner must have been a striking structure: its foundation has bossed polygonal masonry of durable limestone while the walls show regular courses of softer limestone. These details and the round shape of the tower indicate that the tower was built at a time when it was necessary to protect oneself from missiles, that is, not before the 3rd century BCE. About 50m to the east of this tower is another semicircular tower built with exactly the same technique; thus, we see that in the Hellenistic period special arrangements for defence had to be

Fig. 40 Northeast Gate, present state.

made in the area where the Northeast Gate is located. The road network connecting the Lykian cities is not known clearly or fully; however, the geography indicates that this gate opened to the road leading to the cities on the left bank of the River Xanthos – that is, Tlos and Patara. Perhaps, the city of Xanthos was afraid of attacks from this side...

Continuing along a small path winding through the bushes, one leaves the walls behind and a large necropolis flanking an ancient road whose route is unknown runs towards the east, up to the next hill in the distance. In this necropolis there are several interesting Lykian tombs from the 4th century BCE and Roman sarcophagi further ahead.

Sarcophagus with Lions Devouring a Bull (21)

There are two very important Lykian tombs on the slope. The first is a monumental tomb with a depiction of lions devouring a bull (Fig. 41). It is in a bad state and only part of the chest – its Lykian inscription is legible partially – and foundation have survived. The pillar is cut from the bedrock, like the Sarcophagus of the Dancers (18), and is decorated with superb figures in relief and dated to the 4th century BCE from the style. A bull lying in the middle is flanked by two lions that are about to devour him. The animals are depicted with great elegance and a lot of litheness in their movements. Especially the details of the lion on the right hand side, putting his paw on the bull to push him down are noteworthy. Though this relief reflects Hellenized style, the theme

Fig. 41 Sarcophagus with lions devouring a bull (4th century BCE). Detail from the reliefs on the base.

of lions attacking a bull is of Oriental origin. Thus, here we have a product reflecting a blend of cultures, which was produced during the time when Xanthos was under Persian rule.

Closer to the fortifications and further up the slope, there are traditional Lykian rock-cut tombs imitating timber architecture. Despite their interesting look, they are less important than the Lykian necropolis at the acropolis of Xanthos or the rock-cut tombs at other Lykian towns such as Myra and Limyra.

Bibliography: P. Demargne, FdeX, V.

Merehi Tomb (22)

Further away from the fortifications to the north, in the midst of bushes one suddenly comes across a large Lykian sarcophagus, looking as if was toppled down by a giant (in fact it was plunderers). Its lid, decorated with fabulous reliefs, was taken to London by Charles Fellows in the 19th century. On the long side there are hunting scenes of a panther and Chimaira and on the ridge beam are combat and banquet scenes.

To the east, there are numerous Roman sarcophagi, mostly broken by plunderers, in the necropolis on the hill on the other side of the valley. Their layout indicates vaguely the routes of the roads to Patara (to the south) or Tlos (to the north). About 1 km to the east is a Roman *heroon* in ruins and covered with vegetation.

Bibliography: P. Demargne, FdeX, V.

NECROPOLIS ON THE HILL

Returning to the city and entering the Acropolis via the North Gate (20), the beautiful necropolis of Xanthos lies before us. In this area the visitor will find examples of all three tomb types of the Classical Lykian period: pillar tombs, sarcophagi and rock tombs (Fig. 42).

Pillar Tomb on the Acropolis (23)

P. Demargne observed that the "Pillar Tomb on the Acropolis" was the last of such tombs built by Xanthians and was probably erected in the 4th century BCE (Fig.s 42 and 43). It has striking dimensions: the total height is 7.49m, the monolithic pillar measures 2.28m wide by 2.43m long by 4.75m tall. The burial chamber was formed with white marble slabs, with exceptional polishing 1.13m in height, which shows that they were not meant for decoration in relief. Therefore, it seems that they were intended to be painted or were painted but nothing from this painted decoration has survived. The burial chamber is taller than perceived because the monolithic pillar was carved hollow to a depth of 1.15m from the top. Adding the height of the marble slabs, the burial chamber reaches a depth of 2.28m, with a width of 1.90m and a length of 2.09m. No trace of a burial was found.

Rock-cut Tombs

Beneath the Pillar Tomb on the Acropolis (23) are interesting rock-cut tombs of considerable dimensions, which have survived in a good state because they were concealed from the eyes; they were buried (Fig. 44).

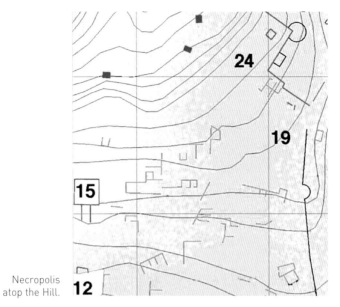

Necropolis
atop the Hill.

Fig. 42 North Necropolis, general view. Pillar Tomb on the Acropolis stands over the rock-tombs.

Fig. 43 North Necropolis, "the Pillar Tomb on the Acropolis". (4th century BCE).

As would be expected, the façades of these tombs imitate timber architecture, and if examined carefully it will be seen that the craftsmanship is extraordinary in the finest detail, even the wooden wedges are imitated, that they were sculpted rectilinearly and polished excellently. Further down from is another tomb, which has some horizontal protuberances at the bottom, suitable for placing some sort of lean-to roof. Blocks belonging to the horizontal lid imitating tree trunks lie scattered around. On these protuberances are mortise holes for placing the lateral supports of the lean-to roof. The mortises are shallow holes for fitting tenons of stone, which were all procured from the same body of rock. This technique of working the stone was typical of the classical Lykian period between the 6th and the 4th centuries BCE.

Looking into the tombs we see roughly worked inner chambers concealed by these fine façades. In the simple chambers cut from the rock are benches to place the corpses. It was customary to put gifts along with the bodies but nothing has survived from any of these plundered tombs. Since they were family tombs, they had doorways that could be reopened in order to place someone else who died later. The bones of a long dead person could be pushed to the side to make room for the newcomer.

Despite the destruction on its façade the rock tomb further up is particularly interesting (Fig. 45). This tomb, the last one of the group on the left, has a different look, imitating a Greek façade of Ionic style and still retains the bases of the columns *in antis* and the corners of the pediment. All these elements and the frame of the doorway to the burial chamber were cut from the same rock. The inscription in ancient Lykian language to the right of the

Fig. 44 Northeast Necropolis, façade of rock-cut tomb (4th century BCE).

Fig. 45   Northeast Necropolis, Façade of Ionic tomb. (2nd half of 4th century BCE).

doorway gives the identity of the deceased as Memruwi, son of Khentcnuba, and announces that anybody attempting to bury somebody not from this family should be fined 3 *ada* (Lykian coin with a value not known). The Hellenized style of this tomb suggests a date younger than other tombs at the necropolis – second half of the 4th century BCE.

If you climb the rock behind the pillar tomb you will find a Lykian tomb left unfinished for reasons unknown.

Bibliography: P. Demargne, FdeX, I.

Payava (Pajava) Tomb (24)

Near the group of rock tombs described above is the strange looking pillar of a monument deprived of its decoration. A superb sarcophagus of multiple tiers surmounting the pillar was the tomb of a Xanthian called Payava (Pajava) who died around 370 - 350 BCE, as its inscription tells us. The chest and lid of the sarcophagus and the reliefs on its pillar were transported to London in the 19th century. The monument, "certainly the largest and the most beautiful one of Classical Lykian sarcophagi" as attested by P. Demargne, comprised several tiers: a three stepped *crepis*, a *hyposorion* still in situ but deprived of its decoration in relief, an intermediary lid (still *in situ*), a massive pillar (still *in situ*), the sarcophagus imitating timber architecture, and an ogival lid with protuberances in the form of lion heads (Fig. 46). The total height of this spectacular monument reached 7.85 m.

The iconography of figures in low relief is particularly rich noteworthy among those on the pillar are: hunting and combat scenes on the ridge beam; sphinxes and antithetic couples placed in frames imitating timber architecture on the short sides of the lid; depictions of quadrigas on the long sides; a combat scene and an audience scene. An incomplete inscription not yet fully deciphered reads: "This chruvata (=?), gave the Persian Satrap Autophradates..." Autophradates is well known by historians and thus confirms the date of the monument.

There is another interesting sarcophagus (Fig. 47) a little further down from the Payava Tomb. Despite its more humble dimensions, it is preserved in its entirety, presenting all the characteristics of Lykian architecture. When we compare this monument with a modern Lykian granary (Fig. 48), it is easy to see a style of architecture that has survived in the countryside of Lykia since antiquity.

Bibliography: P. Demargne, FdeX, V.

Fig. 46   Payava Tomb (computer image, D. Laroche).

Fig. 47 Northeast Necropolis, Lykian sarcophagus imitating Lykian timber architecture (4th century BCE).

Fig. 48 Modern Lykian granary (Elmalı region in north Lykia).

Ahqqadi Tomb (25)

To the west of the group of tombs described above, half the way up the hill, a small path branches away. 50 meters along this small path is a Lykian sarcophagus intact except for its contents. Conforming to the arrangement in tiers of the great Lykian sarcophagi the monument comprises a stepped foundation, a hyposorion, horizontal lid, sarcophagus and lid. Reaching a total height of 6.91 meters the tomb is made of stone polished perfectly and does not have decoration in relief. However, there are lion heads on both sides of the lid to facilitate lifting. It does not have the usual timber architecture imitation. The inscription (in good condition) on the north side begins: "ebêñne : prñnawã : me-ne : prñnawate Ahqqadi..." which translates as: "this house was built by Ahqqadi, son of Pizibide and nephew of Embromos. And the people charged him 10.5 *ada*

LYKIAN TOMBS

Vestiges of funeral architecture form the most curious aspect of Lykian archaeology: some Lykian monuments, such as pillar tombs, are not found elsewhere and also have very particular forms imitating timber architecture. The most famous monuments are the pillar tombs formed by an enormous monolithic pillar (4 to 5m tall and 2.40m wide and weighing 20 to 30 tons) surmounted with the burial chamber. These pillars – the tombs of local rulers from 6th through 4th centuries BCE – are found all over Lykia and the biggest group is in Xanthos.

Lykian tombs (from left to right): Harpy's Tomb, Inscribed Pillar, Pillar Tomb with a Sarcophagus, House-type Tomb, Rock-cut Tomb,

Other Lykian tombs are rock-cut, house-type and sarcophagi, all in stone; yet they all have a common feature: these stone structures imitated timber constructions. In this region timber architecture is still in use today and there are examples of timber constructions similar to those imitated by the funeral architecture of the ancient Lykians.

The influence of Greek art caused the indigenous Lykian forms to disappear; the Nereid Monument is actually a pillar tomb entirely transformed into a Greek style temple.

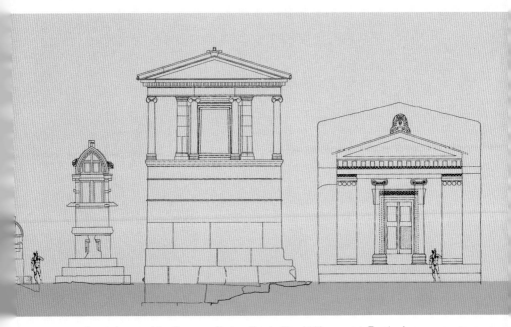

Sarcophagus of the Dancers, Payava Tomb, Nereid Monument, Tomb of Amyntas (in Fethiye) design by G. Verninas.

and for the lower burial chamber 3.5 *ada*. And he gave the upper chamber to his wife and descendants of Menneteidi and he gave the lower chamber to the people of his house."

This beautiful monument provides us with important information on Lykian funeral rites. The burial chambers are spared for certain people, determined beforehand according to rules unknown to us but it is thought that this arrangement depended on the importance of the people, and the immunity of the deceased was kept under guarantee by an official establishment called *miñti*. This tomb can be dated to the first half of the 4th century BCE.

Bibliography: P. Demargne, FdeX, V.

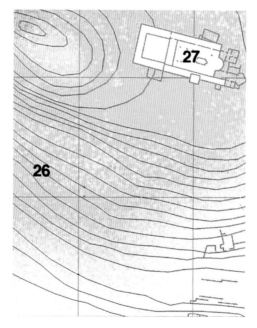

Upper City.

UPPER CITY

The upper city was founded on the slopes of the hill above the city. On the very top are the still imposing ruins of the basilica. The scant remains of the houses on the slopes await courageous visitors. They can be visited on the way back from the Ahqqadi Tomb and afford a magnificent view of the Lower City – especially the Agora, Theatre and the Lykian Acropolis.

Tomb of Aurelios (26)

This visit will also allow us to see a rock tomb on the west slope of the hill above over the Agora. The façade of this recently discovered rock tomb was built in front of the rock-cut burial chamber. The inscription on a block and fragments belonging to the façade tell us the tomb was reused in the 3rd century CE as the last resting place of the family of a man called Aurelios.

Pilgrimage Basilica (27)

There is a big Byzantine church on the summit of the hill. This consists of an atrium partially hewn from the bedrock and a three aisled basilica whose walls are in very good condition. A triconch annex and exterior porticoes leaned on to the side walls of the church. Two big cisterns cut into the rock flanked the church on both sides. Column capitals with egg motif, doorjambs and lintels of Roman period, with fine workmanship, are seen lying in the church. There is no ornamentation on the walls or on the arches; only small marble fragments of various colours belonging to columns and facings hint at the one-time splendour and elegance of the church.

It is hard to give a date for this edifice because there are no certain clues at hand. Based on its location atop the hill, it seems to be a pilgrimage place rather than a regular church. It is possible that it was built in the 6th century, as were most of the Christian structures at Xanthos.

Bibliography: H. Canbilen – J.P. Sodini, AnatAnt. IV, 285-315.

ENVIRONS OF XANTHOS

Aqueduct (28)

Near the modern road past the necropolis, not the Fethiye – Kaş road, there are the traces of an aqueduct from Roman times, not very appealing, to tell the truth. Preserved to the height of two courses of limestone, it still has the traces of the water canal here and there. Researchers were able to follow the aqueduct up to İslamlar village in the mountaneous region to the east of Xanthos. The total length of the aqueduct is 7 km.

Bibliography: J. Burdy – P. Lebouteiller, L'aqueduc romain de Xanthos, AnatAnt., VI, 1998, 227-248.

Long Wall (29)

Just as seen occasionally in other parts of the ancient world, the Xanthians built a Long Wall on the right bank of River Xanthos cutting communication across the valley (Fig. 49). To reach this interesting wall follow the route to the aqueduct. Past Çavdır village, turn north. Passing through a pine forest, one reaches Palamut village. Those travelling by car need to leave their car 500 metres before entering the village and proceed into the fields on the left. Continuing westward, the first part of the wall will come into sight. This wall comes down from the east slope of the valley, crosses the valley and goes up the north slope of a hill and continues downstream along the River Xanthos. The total length of the wall is 3 km. A branch leaving the main wall goes around the top of the hill. On this branch,

Fig. 49 The Long Wall of Xanthos. (5th century BCE).

a few terrace walls and traces of a rectangular structure near the top of the hill have been found. A bit further is a curious structure cut into the rock. It is a structure arranged in tiers, similar to a square milestone; a hole was opened on its top. Its function is still a mystery.

The Long Wall was obviously built for defence. However, the date and exact purpose of this Long Wall connecting to a hill and thus, blocking the whole valley, are shrouded in mist. The scarcity of potsherds and lack of repair marks or annexes suggest that the Long Wall was used only for a short period of time. The wall was built with unworked big stones except for a short section of polygonal masonry with slightly finer workmanship; it can be dated roughly to the 6th or 5th century BCE. Neither any military danger during this period, nor other serious threat that could justify the construction of such a massive wall has been determined.

Bibliography: J. des Courtils – Th. Marksteiner, AnatAnt, VII, 1999, 89-104.

FORTS ON THE WEST BANK: BÜKSES, PYDNAI

On the north side of the Xanthos estuary, there are two archaeological sites on a pretty beach road. To reach them, take the road to Letoon and then turn right towards Karadere, a small village at the foot of the mountains bounding the Xanthos plain on the west.

Bükses (30)

Past Karadere watch out for Bükses Fort, whose ancient name is not known and which stands about 100m away from the road.

Only a terrace surrounded with a wall of 5 - 6m in height has survived of the fort. There must have been some other buildings of lighter construction but nothing has reached the present day. The walls supporting the terrace were built with very large stones. Since there have been no excavations here, we can date it to the 5th century BCE based only on the stone masonry of the walls. Though we lack any information on the function of the fort, a second construction to be discussed below will suggest an explanation for both.

Pydnai (31)

The name of Pydnai Fort comes from inscriptions at the site. Pydnai is the name of the fort in antiquity; however, in the inscriptions, it is mentioned also as Kydnai. Comparable to Bükses Fort, Pydnai Fort, too, is located by a small creek, at a slight elevation compared to the plain (Fig. 50). However, here is a totally Greek fortress from the 3rd century BCE. This date corresponds to the period when Lykia, along with entire south coast of Anatolia, was under the rule of Ptolemies Hellenistic dynasty of Egypt. The structure has survived in very good condition.

The fort comprises a wall over 300 meters in length fortified with square towers (Fig. 51). Towers and walls reach a height of 10 meters at places. Staircases providing access to the walkway along the top of the curtain wall are still *in situ*. The walls were built with bossed polygonal masonry technique characteristic to the beginning of the Hellenistic Era and present a good example of well preserved structures of the same period.

There is access to the interior from the northwest. The interior of the fort is empty except for a small church in ruins. This building proves that the fort was used by the Christians living around to take refuge. There must have been other buildings of lighter construction on the inside. From the dimensions of the fort we know that it was under constant guard and was an important centre.

This fort was built to guard the coast of Xanthos. In fact, the only safe place to anchor vessels was by Pydnai. Winds and currents rendered the Lykian coasts dangerous but Pydnai was protected by a rocky promontory so the sea was calm here.

Fig. 50 Pydnai Fort (3rd century BCE)
(drawing by J.-P. Adam, colouring by G. Verninas).

Moreover, a small creek flowing into the sea nearby was an invaluable source of fresh water, hard to find along the coast. Sailors were able to get fresh water here. Geomorphological research shows that the sea has been retreating since antiquity so Pydnai Fort must have been located right on the coast when it was built; the garrison must have been on guard all the time.

The same is true for Bükses Fort as well. When it was built, Bükses must have been very close to the coast and just like Pydnai, protected from the winds and close to the river. As the sea retreated, Bükses, too, was left in the middle of mainland.

The estuary between Xanthos and the sea was an impassable marshland. So attackers had to anchor by these stronghold points. To reach Xanthos from the coast, one had to follow the

Fig. 51
Pydnai.
Tower on the
south side.

foot of the hills, which in turn were guarded by these two forts. In the late Roman times Xanthos was connected to the coast via a road around the marsh. A military border mark from the Tetrarchy period at the end of the 3rd century CE found at Karadere village shows that an important Roman road passed here. The road between the marsh and the hills was meant to connect the safe port to Xanthos (and also the Letoon Sanctuary).

Bibliography: J.-P. Adam, L'Architecture militaire grecque.

VISIT TO LETOON

Letoon is 5 km as the crow flies from Xanthos. The modern road is different from that of antiquity: the old road ran downstream along the right bank of the river and changed direction about the Kumluova village. Visitors from Xanthos arrived at the slope where the theatre is located to the north of the sanctuary proper. The modern road reaches the foot of the hill above Letoon.

LEGEND OF THE SANCTUARY

The name of Letoon comes from the name of the goddess Leto. Here the goddess Leto was worshiped with her twins from Zeus, Artemis and Apollo. According to the legend, as soon as Leto gave birth to her twins, she left Delos to escape the wrath of Hera, wife of Zeus, and arrived in Lykia. She wanted to get some water from the springs here for her twins but the local shepherds did not let her because they were afraid of Hera. So, Leto became angry and turned them into frogs. In time a cult of the goddess and her twins was founded at the site where this took place.

This legend is a wealth of information. First of all, we see that this area was abundant with water even in antiquity. Moreover, a different aspect of the cult also emerges: though the deities mentioned above belong to the Greek pantheon, they were disguised in a very non-Hellenic form here. In the legend, Leto is the foremost deity whereas in the Greek pantheon her twins, Artemis and Apollo, are more important and Leto has a more humble place. In addition, Apollo does not visit this sanctuary and does not communicate through oracles here. Whereas, he used to come to Delphoi in Greece and Didyma, Klaros and Patara temples in Turkey. Thus the temple before us was dedicated not to a god but to a goddess, a goddess of water. The goddess is surrounded with water fairies *(nymphe)* called *Elyana*s in the Lykian language. This goddess was "modernised" with the introduction of Greek gods. It is thought that the cult was Hellenized by the local potentate Arbinas who lived around the end of the 5th century BCE, because numerous inscriptions recovered during the course of excavations prove that this person was directly involved on the cult. The fact that one of them was written in Greek is a sign of Hellenization, and the construction of the Temple of Leto is also attributed to Arbinas.

HISTORY OF THE SANCTUARY

The history of the sanctuary did not develop parallel to that of the city, as their natures were different. Xanthos was a city and Letoon was a religious sanctuary. Furthermore, Letoon though dependent on the city, was at times a federal sanctuary of the whole Lykian people.

According to archaeologists, the history of Letoon starts at the same time as Xanthos: some pots recovered very deep confirm the presence of people here about 700 BCE. In the north of the sanctuary, we find important layout and annexes built later beneath the porticoes seen today. When the underground water table falls more than usual, vague traces of these early buildings can be seen among the columns of later porticoes.

In the beginning, Leto was a rural cult centre. The centre of the Elyana cult was a spring coming from under a hill in the midst of the marshland plains of the Xanthos estuary. Elyanas were water goddesses and later identified with the nymphs of ancient Greek religion. A few structures of the 5th century BCE, entirely in ruins, are all that remain of the earliest sanctuary.

The sanctuary probably started to gain importance at the end of the 5th century during the reign of the potentate Arbinas. Temples dedicated to three deities, Leto, Artemis and Apollo, were built in this period. One of the inscriptions recovered in the sanctuary bears the claim by Arbinas that he inaugurated the Artemis cult here and also built the Temple of Leto. These are Greek deities even though they are related with the Anatolian ones. It is likely that Arbinas also initiated the cult of Apollo because it is reasonable that the cults of three deities (Leto and her twins) started simultaneously. However, there is still one point not clear: they might have been identified with the local deities or they might have been enforced by a ruler. An ivory figurine recovered in north Lykia – now on display at Antalya Museum – depicts a woman holding a girl and a boy. If this is a religious figurine – it probably is – then it provides us with a very important proof of the existence of an early triad that was Hellenized in the reign of Arbinas. However, we lack evidence to prove this with certainty for the moment.

It is certain that the Letoon Sanctuary underwent development after the 4th century BCE and became a magnificent monument in the early years of the Hellenistic Era: particularly the three temples in the Hellenistic style, porticoes encircling the sanctuary and the theatre. There probably was also a stadium, but its whereabouts has not yet been discovered. There has been no work done in the south side of the sanctuary. It is certain that some of these structures were built for the Romaia-Letoia festivals, as the sanctuary was developed as federal sanctuary of the Lykian League. As religion and politics were strongly linked in antiquity, Letoon was the symbolic centre of Lykia and official documents were also kept here. Numerous official texts from this period have been recovered in the course of excavations.

Letoon underwent various changes in the Roman times. Though Lykia shrank in size as a province, and therefore, the sanctuary did lose its importance to a small degree, its religious quality was retained. New structures such as an imperial hall for the cult of the emperors and a monumental fountain dedicated to Hadrian were added in this period.

With the spread of Christianity a church was built here in the 6th century. The temples of Apollo and Artemis were dismantled and their material was probably reemployed for the construction of the church. The Temple of Leto stood a bit longer (perhaps served the Christian cult); yet, it could not escape destruction at the hand of mankind. However, its material was not even reused somewhere else because the sanctuary was soon abandoned until its rediscovery in 1840. Systematic and regular excavations started in 1962 and still continue focusing on the restoration of the Temple of Leto.

Bibliography: C. Le Roy, Dossiers de l'Archeologie, December 1998, s. 42-50.

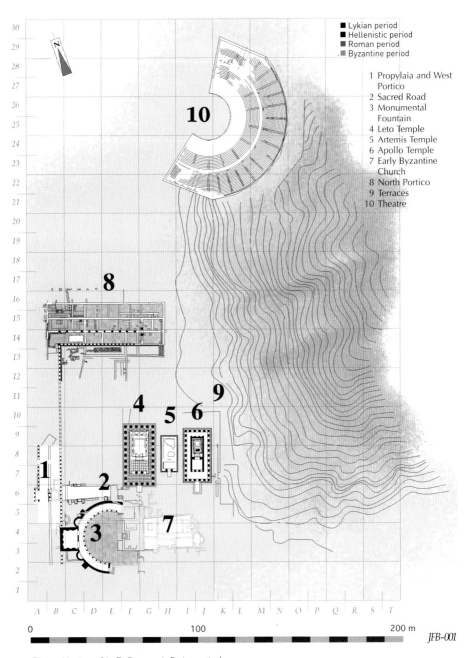

■ Lykian period
■ Hellenistic period
■ Roman period
■ Byzantine period

1 Propylaia and West Portico
2 Sacred Road
3 Monumental Fountain
4 Leto Temple
5 Artemis Temple
6 Apollo Temple
7 Early Byzantine Church
8 North Portico
9 Terraces
10 Theatre

JFB-001

Plan of Letoon (J.-F. Bernard, D. Laroche).

VISITING THE SANCTUARY

There is no information to hand regarding the boundaries of the sanctuary in antiquity. On the east, it is bounded with terraces at the foot of the hill. The eastern and northern boundaries are provided by porticoes. The theatre was added later to the north, outside the first boundary of the sanctuary. A sounding confirms that the sanctuary lies at least 50m to the south (towards the sea). Perhaps the stadium, whose existence is known from the inscriptions recovered, will be located in this section.

The entrance gate to the ruins is at a different spot than the original main entrance to the sanctuary. Today visitors reach the site from behind the temples. Visitors with limited time may visit the theatre and the three temples only. Those with plenty of time should visit clockwise the theatre, elevated terraces, temples, Early Christian Basilica, *nymphaion, propylons (propylaia)*, and porticoes.

Theatre (10)

The best preserved structure at the site, the theatre is also one of the most interesting (Fig. 52). The excavations here have not been completed but we know that the theatre was built around the middle of the 2nd century BCE.

The stage building is entirely in ruins but its location has been spotted three meters below the ground. Only the rows of seats *(koilon)* are in good condition and still *in situ* from the bottom to the top. The middle part was hewn from the bedrock and the right and left wings were built using the stones quarried out. A

Fig. 52 Letoon Theatre (2nd century BCE).

total of 36 rows of seats were divided horizontally into two by a *diazoma* and vertically into 11 *kerkides* by stairs. The tunnels reaching the *diazoma* are a noteworthy feature of this Hellenistic theatre: the one on the north is located at the end of the road coming from Xanthos and the one on the south connected the theatre to the sanctuary.

Visitors are advised to go through the vaulted north tunnel to the *diazoma*. Before entering the corridor we can see an interesting lid of a Lykian sarcophagus amidst the blocks of rows of seats scattered by an earthquake. This lid proves the existence of a cemetery on this spot before the construction of the theatre. There are other tombs by the exit of the tunnel; a sarcophagus carved from the bedrock and its lid added later on is especially noteworthy. The relief decorating the sarcophagus depicts a widespread theme – a person reclining at a feast. The next one is not of any particular interest. The presence of all these tombs in this area is especially worth noting for in antiquity it was customary to have tombs flank the roads. So we can see that the people coming from Xanthos may have arrived at Letoon through here. This land was marsh in antiquity and not usable; so the road at the foot of the hill had to be elevated from the surrounding area.

Because the road from the city to the sanctuary ended here there was richer decoration on the exterior wall of the theatre at this point. Niches were built on both sides of the entrance to the tunnel but it is not known whether the statues were ever made. There is a capping in Doric composite style, i.e. with an Ionic architrave and a Doric frieze, above the entranceway to the tunnel. The *metopes* of the frieze are decorated with theatre masks in relief. The theatre masks were very important because they helped the audience to easily recognise the characters in the play.

As we have seen, the rows of seats were built on an already existing tomb. This suggests that the theatre was built on the road leading to the sanctuary. Thus, the diazoma was planned to be an access way as well. So, the visitors entered via the gate, passed the masks, continued along the diazoma and passed through the other tunnel. We will use the same way to reach the sanctuary, just as the ancient Lykians did centuries ago.

Leaving the theatre through the south corridor we can have a look at the decoration on this side. This decoration is also attractive, yet less fine. The architect built a Doric pediment over the vault (Fig. 53), which does have an elegant look indeed.

Now visit the temples, leaving the theatre to the south and following the elevated terrace.

Bibliography: A. Badie – J.-C. Moretti, AnatAnt. VI, 471-475; VIII, 340-341.

Terraces (9)

The terraces above the sanctuary cover the slope on the east. Looking from here, all the ruins present a beautiful view. The first terrace starts by the south exit of the theatre and probably led to an entranceway of the sanctuary. This was an artificial terrace supported by a wall that no longer exists. From the remains we know that the wall was built with unworked polygonal stones. Along the edge of the terrace on the hillside some buildings were erected but their nature is not known.

Fig. 53 Letoon Theatre, south entrance.

100 meters from the theatre, the terrace makes an elbow and then continues in the original direction. From this point on, the terrace does not rest on a wall but rather is hewn from the bedrock. Reaching the temples' square, the terrace becomes a double terrace: a lower one and a parallel upper one. The lower terrace was formed from rock hewn and polished excellently and its level is 1 meter below the present ground level. There are traces of holes in the rock along the edge of the falaise above the temples. These holes might have belonged to a portico not existing now or to votive offerings such as statues and steles. The upper terrace was hewn from the rock and was partitioned with walls and completed with front walls of brick or stone. These chambers might have been used as a residence or used for religious feasts here. Their date is not known either; however, given the porticoes with excellent right angles, these may also belong to the Hellenistic Period.

TEMPLES' SQUARE

The three temples (Fig.s 54 and 55) make up the most interesting group of monuments in the sanctuary. They are in a flat area hewn from the rock below a man-made falaise. This terrace underwent various alterations and rearrangements in the course of time. When it was originally built, the temples were planned to stand on natural rocks. Thus, the construction of three temples commenced, but later the structures whose remains are visible today, were built in place of the original temples.

In this square there are rare features: all three temples are strictly parallel to each other and to the rocky falaise, and all face south instead of east. Therefore, we see that monumental order was calculated with great rigour. Considering that the lower porticoes also conform to this orthogonal layout, we know that the whole sanctuary was built to a pre-established plan: this is a unique example in the whole Greco-Asian world.

Various modest monuments, such as steles with official texts and statues standing on pedestals, were added in time. There must have been an altar in front of each temple but nothing has survived since a church was built in their place. At a later period surrounding walls were built using blocks from the temples and other structures because the square was exposed to outside; even grain grinding areas were unearthed. All these alterations deeply affected the appearance of the sanctuary.

Bibliography: C. Le Roy, RA 1974, 313-340.

Fig. 54 Letoon. General view of the three temples from north east. From letf to right: Apollo, Artemis ve Leto Temples.

Temple of Apollo (6)

The temple closest to the falaise is that of Apollo in the Doric order. Just like its neighbours, this temple is oriented towards the south. This contrasts with the standard Greek temple, whose façade normally faced to the rising sun. The Temple of Apollo is in ruins down to its foundation. When it was standing in full height, there was a three-stepped *crepis* above the foundation, as seen from the traces on the south. There were 6 columns along the façade and 11 on the long sides. However, only tiny fragments have been recovered of the superstructure of the temple, which

Fig. 55 Letoon. Reconstructed view of the temples from south. From left to right: Leto, Artemis, Apollo Temples (design by D. Laroche).

was totally dismantled, crushed and burned down in kilns to make lime by the occupants in the Byzantine Era. Though they present a poor view, it is interesting and worth going up the remains and examining the inner layout of the edifice.

Going up into the temple, the mosaics on the floor of the *cella* catch the eye. This mosaic pavement can be examined in three sections. The panel on the right is decorated with the motif of a *lyra*, which is appropriate for Apollo, the god of art, who is usually depicted together with this musical instrument. The panel on the left with a depiction of a bow and a quiver recalls to the minds that Apollo was an archer god. The panel in the middle is decorated with a rosette *(rozas)*, which might have been depicted

142

to represent the sun – another symbol of Apollo. This mosaic is the only evidence to identify the god whom this temple was dedicated.

The mosaic clearly dates to the mid 2nd century BCE and it was made as the floor of the pre-existing temple. However, the structure enclosing it contains curious details: the mosaic is placed within some sort of a frame made of larger stones, different from the rest of the floor. The edges of this frame are not parallel to the walls of the temple and run to a line of stones dividing the cella. Finally, there is a groove and numerous rectangular holes placed at regular intervals and at the corners of this structure.

All these unusual and strange details can be explained as follows: in the beginning, the Lykians built the first temple on a rocky outcrop, whose traces can be seen within the foundations of the Doric temple. This first temple was built of timber fixed unto the rock surface through the means of the holes and the groove (Fig. 56). The same construction techniques are seen in modern granaries in Lykia (Fig. 57). Thus, the Temple of Apollo at Letoon is unique evidence that ancient Lykian architecture was of timber. Until this temple was found, the imitation of timber work seen on the stone tombs was put forth as evidence for this hypothesis.

This first timber temple was converted into a Doric temple of stone. However, its orientation was slightly changed for reasons unknown. Yet, the fact that the original timber temple is enclosed and preserved within the Doric temple is extraordinary. The evidence is provided by the only changes – the addition of mosaic into the floor of the first temple and the replacement of the

Fig. 56 Apollo Temple. Traces of the Lykian structure inside the cella.

Fig. 57 Detail from the modern Lykian granary.

threshold. Thus, the first temple had a function within the second temple, a remarkable example of smart religious policy. The first temple built with local traditional architecture is conserved as a holy relic and sheltered within a new temple built with Greek inspiration and model.

Unfortunately, it is not possible to determine the exact dates of the various phases in this history; the first phase may be much older (maybe 5th century) and the Doric temple may be from the 4th century or the beginning of Hellenistic Era, and the addition of mosaics in the 2nd century may correspond to a date like 166 BCE when Lykia was released from the Rhodian yoke.

Bibliography: C. Llinas, RA, 1974, 313-340.

"Trilingual Inscription of Letoon"

A rectangular stele bearing an inscription, on display at Fethiye Museum today, was recovered between the Temple of Apollo and the falaise in 1979 and is an exceptional document. There are inscriptions on two wide and one narrow face of this intact stele. The texts on the wide faces are identical and one is in Greek while the other is in Lykian (Fig. 58). There is a summary in Aramaic on the narrow face. The find is dated to 337 BCE.

The text records a special donation in the name of a goddess by the "Basileios Kaunios" (King of Kaunos), who is also known from other sources and the Inscribed Pillar at Xanthos (2). The terms and conditions mentioned in the text provided historians with new information on the administrative and religious structures of Lykia and especially Xanthos.

This find of considerable significance helped greatly in the research of Lykian language because the texts in Greek and Lykian arc identical. However, the short text on the narrow side was no help.

Bibliography: H. Metzger – E. Laroche, A. Dupont-Sommer – M. Mayrhoffer, FdeX, VI, 1979; P. Briant, CRAI, 1998, 305-347.

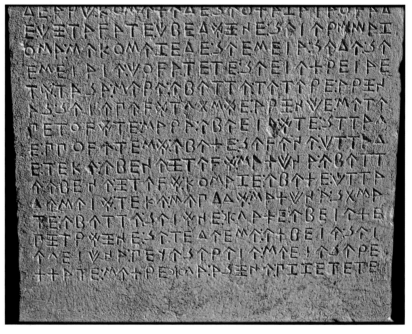

Fig. 58 The Letoon Trilingual Inscription, the text in Lykian (Fethiye Museum).

Temple of Artemis (5)

The Temple of Artemis is in a worse condition than the Apollo Temple but there is enough evidence to reconstruct its more or less similar story (Fig. 59).

The identity of the monument is established by two inscriptions. One is protected at the excavation house depot and is a dedication to Artemis by the potentate Arbinas from about 400/380 BCE. It was found to the left of the temple entrance. The other is an inscription on a statue base to the right of the entrance still *in situ*. This text starts in Greek and is completed in Lykian, stating that a Demokleides (Ntemukhlida in Lykian) born in Limyra (Zemuri in Lykian) presented a statue to the goddess Artemis. It is dated to ca. 360 BCE.

Artemis was honoured at an earlier temple, probably a timber one, which has not survived, like that of her twin brother. The existence of such a temple is shown by the traces on the rock surface in the middle of the ruin. The edges of this rock are not parallel to the later temple enclosing it but rather parallel to the sides of the first Temple of Apollo and this indicates that it underwent similary alterations.

The second Temple of Artemis was not preserved any better than that of Apollo. The Temple, dismantled entirely in the 5th or 6th century, was of Ionic (or Corinthian) order and originally had 4 columns in front while there were no columns along the lateral sides or the rear side. Therefore, it was a prostyle or had two columns *in antis*. A few small finds (we have to note that they are smaller than an egg), that have survived, betray that the temple had a particular architectural quality: mouldings of outstanding

Fig. 59 Artemis Temple, front: Demokleides base.

elegance and finishing (Fig. 60). We can judge by looking at the entablature, a floral frieze of palmettes and lotuses following each other, and an architrave of three *fasciae*.

This stone temple can be dated to the reign of Arbinas (beginning of the 4th century BCE) from the inscriptions. It is not possible to date precisely the first temple built with timber.

Fig. 60 Artemis Temple, cyma fragment.

Temple of Leto (4)

As Leto was the chief deity here, her temple was of course larger than the others. The temple was destroyed in the 7th century CE, probably due to an earthquake but evidence also indicates that part of the destruction was intentional. A short while after the destruction the area was totally abandoned; therefore, the material was not plundered to a great deal in order to be used elsewhere and most stayed in place.

Only the foundations and the lower parts of the walls of the temple have survived but hundreds of blocks lying in the north part of the site belong to this temple (Fig. 61). These blocks have been collected and aligned on the ground since 1972 by the excavation teams first under the direction of H. Metzger and then under C. Le Roy. In the south section columns and entablature fragments were left where they were (Fig. 62). Thanks to the abundance of material at hand, it has been possible to reconstruct the temple in detail (Fig. 63).

Fig. 61   Leto Temple, at the onset of the excavations (1964).

The Temple of Leto was a peripteral of Ionic order, with 6 columns along the short and 11 columns along the long sides. The Ionic capitals have very fine workmanship. The entablature, an architrave and a polished frieze, was crowned with a roof channel with magnificent decoration: palmettes and lotus flowers alternate on top of the fronton and there were gargoyles with lions' heads and foliage along the lateral sides of the building (Fig. 64).

Passing through the colonnade of the façade one reaches the deep *pronaos* with two columns *(distylos) in antis*. The slightly depressed flagstones of the floor pavement here form a sort of basin. The cella, entered through a monumental doorway, had walls accentuated with half-columns with Corinthian capitals, and crowned with a frieze of palmettes and lotuses.

Fig. 62   Leto Temple, western façade today.

Fig. 63   Leto Temple, 3-D reconstruction (D. Laroche).

The interior of the temple is inaccessible but the outcrops of the rock on which the temple was built are visible. On this rock there are still traces of an earlier temple foundation built with polygonal masonry. Perhaps there was a Lykian type timber temple standing on this foundation. It is worth noting that the second temple built to contain the older one never had a floor pavement. This observation proves that the construction was designed to contain the first temple within the second temple. This was true for the Temple of Apollo; and, it may be true for the Temple of Artemis as well.

Unfortunately it is not possible to date the temples of Leto based on the scarce evidence from the excavations. It is not possible to date the first timber temple precisely. However, an interesting inscription found elsewhere mentions that Arbinas, who ruled in the beginning of 4th century BCE, introduced the cult of the goddess here. Yet the timber temple should have been built even earlier. The big temple presents contradicting architectural features: the exterior order can be dated to the 4th century from the style of the decoration. On the contrary, the frieze decoration on the inner sides of the *cella* walls is younger (more or less mid 2nd century). Thus, the temple may have been

Fig. 64   Temple of Leto (4), cyma block.

built twice. Either there was an interruption during construction or the upper parts of the cella walls were restored or repaired at a later date. A coin hoard of mid 2nd century BCE recovered in the temple might be from the time of restoration.

An important program of reconstruction of the Temple of Leto has been initiated under the direction of D. Laroche and J.-F. Bernard and the sponsorship of the Ministry of Foreign Affairs of France.

Bibliography: E. Hansen, Ch. Le Roy, "Au Letoon de Xantos: Les deux temples de Leto", RA, 1976, 317-336.

Early Byzantine Church (7)

To the south of the temples are the remains of a well preserved church of the 6th century CE. The layout of the church can easily be recognised. To the west is a narthex, flanked with rooms of unknown function. The nave is flanked with narrower aisles on both sides. To the southeast is a small triconch structure with a well preserved floor mosaic, which is unusual for it contains an inscription. The phrase "deacon of angels" indicates a liturgy, not known anywhere else; this chamber may have been used for funerals.

The temples of Apollo and Artemis may have been destroyed with the construction of this church in the 6th century. However, the Temple of Leto was not intentionally destroyed in this period. Traces of a corridor connecting the temple to the narthex of the church have been uncovered. Therefore, we can conclude that the temple was used as an auxiliary structure of the Christian church for a while.

Propylaia and the West Portico (1)

The area we are to visit last was, in antiquity, actually the most important entranceway to the sanctuary. It is hard to reconstruct the way the pilgrims followed in antiquity but here we will try to imagine it.

The sanctuary was bounded on the west by a wall curving north to south *(peribolos)* (Fig. 65). Examining the foundations of the structure, the only part that has survived, we can date it to the 4th or maybe 3rd century BCE. Traces uncovered in the course of excavations show that a first *propylon* (monumental gate) was opened in this wall.

The wall functioned as a foundation for the Doric portico on the north and west sides of the sanctuary (Fig. 65). The portico was, in a sense, framing the structures within the sanctuary. Numerous bases and a few column fragments lie scattered around. The presence of a portico within a sanctuary is not surprising; they were quite usual and provided shelter for both the gifts to the altar and the visitors. This Doric portico was built in the 2nd century BCE and rebuilt at the end of 1st century CE. During the renovation, a second portico was added adjoining the first from the back side, on the outside of the sanctuary. Moreover, the entranceway was arranged in a more monumental fashion and a group of 4 columns, intersecting the portico, was accentuated with a pediment as a portal.

The inscriptions on a Roman stele recovered in this area probably dated to earlier times and mentioned the rules to be obeyed within the sanctuary (Fig. 66). It was prohibited to enter the sanctuary with arms or iron accessories or to spend the night in the porticoes!

Fig. 65   Letoon, 3-D reconstruction of the Nymphaion and the West Portico
(D. Laroche).

To the right of the people entering the sanctuary, niches were
built in the portico wall. Only the lower parts of the niches built
with stone are preserved. The upper parts of the wall and niches
built with bricks could not resist the damage of time. The identity
of the person whose statue was erected in the niche was inscribed
on the wall below the niche. These texts show that one group of
statues were commissioned and erected in the 1st century BCE
before the time of Julius Caesar, and another group from the end
of 1st or 2nd century CE was sponsored by a Lucius Apollinaris in
honour of his family.

Observations show that the low lying areas of the sanctuary
were flooded continuously as the underground watertables rose.

Fig. 66 Inscription on a stone stele giving the regulations of the sanctuary (excavation house depot.).

In fact, there are stones placed at the passageways of the *propylaia* in order to prevent the penetration of waters into the sanctuary from outside. However, this was an absurd precaution against an invincible phenomenon!

The porticoes on the west and north sides were destroyed completely in the 4th century CE. The ground of the sanctuary was levelled off at 1 meter above the level of the porticoes. A canal was built at the southwest of Leto Temple with stones from ancient structures, probably to drain the flooding waters, from the spring across the ruins of the porticoes and well outside the sanctuary. These activities, altering the look of the sanctuary entirely were inevitable due to the continuously rising ground waters.

Bibliography: C. Le Roy, RA, 1986, 281-300.

SACRED ROAD AND SACRED SPRING (2)

A road paved with stones connected the Western Propylon to the Temple of Leto (Fig. 67). Its present state indicates a date in Roman times but the stones might have been placed earlier to improve the condition of the road. Bases with no statues today flank the road on both sides; they bear interesting inscriptions in Greek (but are of Roman times). On the west end the road was extended by steps, entirely in ruins today, which provided access up to the level of the temples. In the course of work here, the first step and the foundation of the second step have been uncovered.

A few examples for interesting inscriptions are:

- an *agonistic* inscription on a base of three blocks (by the *propylon*)

- a base with an inscription dedicated to the Emperor Nerva (96-98) (in the middle of the south side of the road)

- a base with an inscription dedicated to the Emperor Traianus (Trajan), erected in homage by the Lykian people a short while after the accession to the throne of the emperor (98-117) 1.75m tall against the first step of the Temple of Leto.

Fig. 67 Letoon, Sacred Road.

At the foot of the Temple of Leto is the spring that gave its name to the sanctuary. Excavations brought to light a section of magnificent pavement in and around which terra cotta figurines from Archaic through Hellenistic periods verifying the nature of the sanctuary have been recovered (Fig.s 68 and 69). These figurines were probably dedicated by the visitors to the first deities of the spring rather than goddess Leto. These deities called *Elyanas* by the Lykians later assumed the name *Nymphes* when the cult at the sanctuary was hellenised.

It is thought that the cult of this spring was abandoned when the great Temple of Leto was built. The new foundations covered the paved section because they were much larger than those of the first timber temple and therefore, restricted the area around the spring. Probably for this reason, a massive construction was started to create the look of a natural spring: to the south of the old spring, in front of the rock from which it sprang, an artificial terrace was built facing the west supported by a beautiful wall in the north-south axis. In the middle of this wall, a few regular courses of which have survived, was an entrance into a vaulted chamber. There was a pool in front. Inside the chamber a bench was built. These structures located on the east of a large pool to the south of the temple are clearly visible. Also the ruins of the vaulted chamber opening to the pool can be seen.

There is also an artificial grotto in this layout. These were quite popular in the Hellenistic period and they usually imitated natural caves. Thus, picturesque cult places were prepared for the Nymphes. The stone bench in the artificial grotto was used to place the Nymphe statues and gifts brought by the pilgrims. In the excavations of the earthfilling of the terrace where the Nymphe

Fig. 68 Archaic figurine from the Sacred spring.

Fig. 69 Hellenistic figurine from the Sacred spring.

grotto was built numerous limestone pieces cut from the stones of the Temple of Leto were found. Thus, it is clear that the construction of the grotto and the relocation of the cult of the Nymphes were realised during the rearrangement of this area.

Bibliography: A. Balland, Les Dossiers de l'Archéologie, December 1998, s. 56-57.

Monumental Fountain (3)

An edifice was built opposite the false grotto of Nymphes in the Roman times. A portico semicircular in shape lined a basin and its columns reflected on the water (Fig. 65 and 70). This basin did not have a pavement or an edge as was the case with that in front of the Nymphe grotto. Here the existence of waterproof foundations with a depth of 3 meters proved that the portico lined a room full of water. On top of the colonnade was an entablature, decorated with foliates, numerous fragments of which have survived (Fig. 71). Behind the middle section of the

Fig. 70 Roman Fountain (2nd century) (design by J.-F. Bernard).

portico was a large hall measuring 10 x 10 meters. There were half moon shaped exedrae framing the doorway. An inscription showed there was a statue of Emperor Hadrianus here erected in 131 CE by the Great Priest of the Lykian Confederation. A female head with a diadem was also recovered during excavations. This beautiful piece of sculpture depicted a princess- perhaps Empress Livia- who had lived years earlier.

Obviously this monument dedicated to Emperor Hadrianus is a sign of devotion, one of many the emperor received in the Hellenic or Hellenized lands within the Roman Empire that he had regularly visited.

Bibliography: A. Balland, Les Dossiers de l'Archéologie, December 1998, s. 56-57.

Fig. 71   Roman Fountain, entablature fragments (2nd century).

NORTH PORTICO (8)

The visit to this part of the ruins is full of misery due to high ground waters and the juxtaposition of several phases on top of each other (Fig. 72). The North Portico is the perpendicular extension of the West Portico but its history and details of construction are totally different.

The Graeco-Roman structure seen today conceals the remains of unidentifiable structures from the 4th, even 5th century BCE. The excavations yielded only foundations at the bottom. All this information indicate a rectangular structure and another structure with multiple rooms. The rectangular structure was placed laterally in relation with its descendants. The function of the larger structure remains unclear.

Fig. 72   North Portico, view from east. Front: Imperial cult hall (2nd century).

The North Portico originaly had a Doric façade as did the West Portico whose extension it formed. Probably both were built at the same time, towards the end of the 2nd century BCE. When the North Portico was damaged in a fire about the end of the 1st century CE, it was rearranged completely. The foundation wall was taken further north and was replaced by a colonnade of Ionic columns of mediocre quality. Lower quality material was used in this construction and columns were built with arc shaped bricks and finished with stucco painted in faux-marble. Behind this second line of columns lay a series of rooms.

The portico presents a very complex situation today. We can easily make out the colonnades of the portico by the Doric and Ionic columns and the aisles formed by them. To the front, the great foundation probably supported statues that have not survived. Behind the portico there were many rooms with doors opening outside the sanctuary (to the north). We do not have evidence to determine the functions of these rooms but we can possibly consider at least one of them as a dining hall.

It seems that there were structures to the west of this portico, not visible today, with various special functions. The colours of the mosaic pavement on the floor of the room at the northwest of this portico were kept brilliant under a thin layer of water via a special arrangement. The statue bases in this room were placed across from each other. The presence of statues here proves the existence of a cult dedicated to important people around the beginning of the imperial period. Amongst these notables are Lucius and Caius Caesar, Augustus' step sons who died at a young age. In the adjoining hall is an excellent decoration of bull's heads and garlands on a limestone base (Fig. 73). This

base from Augustus' reign (end of the 1st century BCE) was possibly an altar or a statue base.

A hall at the other end of the portico, the east end, runs the whole breadth of both aisles of the portico. In front of it are bases which once supported bronze statues. When they were uncovered, a foot was still on its base. In the hall, the name of Marciana, sister of Traianus (beginning of the 2nd century CE) was inscribed on a base. Adding one clue to the other, we can see that this hall was used as "ethnikon kaisareion" or "Temple of the Emperors", an inscription recovered at Letoon mentions such a place. Thus, this was the place where the Lykians worshiped the Roman imperial cult.

In the course of excavations thousands of pieces belonging to statues that were broken and reused in the constructions were recovered. This gigantic puzzle was put together after a meticulous effort and the pieces belonged to at least 14 different statues. Six of them were repaired almost completely and are on display at Antalya Museum. These statues of men and women mostly belong to the 1st century BCE and were probably produced at the workshops at Kos. Neither the identities nor the original locations of the statues have been determined. However, it is exciting to think that they once stood on the bases supported by the foundation still visible in front of the North and West porticoes.

Bibliography: H. Metzger et al, FdeX, IX.

GLOSSARY

Acropolis (Acropole) Upper city. In ancient Greek cities, the inner castle was the highest place and was the most suitable place for defence.

Agonistic Related to the organisation of big religious festivals.

Antae The extensions of the lateral walls of ancient Greek temple architecture.

Architrave The lowest part of the superstructure supported by columns. Usually it is linear.

Atrium Courtyard. The inner court of Roman residences or the courtyard flanked with colonnades between the church and the street.

Basilica A type of structure longitudinal rectangle in shape with a roof supported by parallel pillars.

Bouleuterion (Bouleuterium) The building where the advisory council of the city met.

Cardo In ancient Roman cities, the main street in the north-south direction, intersecting with Decumanus at the centre.

Cella (Naos) the holy hall which housed the cult statue in ancient pagan temples.

Chiton A costume in ancient Greece, made by sewing the opposite edges of a rectangular piece of fabric.

Corinthian A class of ancient architecture, recognised by its column capitals with floral (acanthus) decoration accentuated with light and dark.

Cornice A moulding at the top of a façade or separating the floors.

Cryptoporticus Vaulted structures under the ground in ancient Roman architecture.

Decumanus In ancient Roman cities, the main street in the east-west direction, intersecting with Cardo at the centre.

Diadem	A type of crown in the form of a wreath.
Dipylon	A type of Roman triumphal arch formed by two pillars and a single arch.
Distylos in antis	A type of temple with two columns in between the antae.
Doric	The oldest order in ancient architecture. Recognised by columns with no bases and very plain capitals.
Dromos	A long narrow corridor that provided access to the burial chamber in tombs.
Entablature	The whole of the superstructure supported by columns in ancient architecture.
Exedra	A semicircular room, surmounted by a semidome, opening directly into a larger room.
Fascia	In the Ionic and Corinthian order of ancient architecture, band-like horizontal sections of the architrave.
Fresco	Mural painting applied directly on wet plaster.
Frieze	Any work of art in the form of a band decorated with reliefs.
Hellenes	All the ancient Greek-speaking peoples who migrated from mainland of what is Greece today to Anatolia, the Asiatic part of Turkey today (Dorians, Aiolians and Ionians).
Hellenistic Era	The Hellenizing period following Alexander the Great (333 - 33 BCE).
Heroon	An edifice for the honour of venerated heros.
Hoplite	A soldier with heavy arms.
Hyposorion	A tomb at a lower level or under the ground.
in antis	(Latin) between the antae.
Ionic	An architectural order recognised by column capitals with volutes (reminding of ram's horns) and egg-and-dart motif in between.

Kerkis	(Kerkides pl.; cunei Lat.) In ancient theatres, rows of seats between the radial stairs.
Koilon	The seating in ancient theatres.
Kore	Statue of a young girl.
Krepis	(crepis) The steps of the platform on which a temple stood.
Metope	In the Doric order, a rectangular panel, decorated in relief, found between the triglyphs.
Narthex	The entrance foyer in a church between the nave and the atrium or the street.
Necropolis	Cemetery.
Nymphaion	(Nymphaeum) monumental fountains dedicated to the Nymphes.
Opus sectile	A type of floor pavement or wall revetment, made of marble/stone pieces in different colours cut in various shapes and put together.
Orchestra	The low lying area in front of a stage building and surrounded by the koilon on three sides.
Pantheon	All the gods in a pagan religion.
Pelests	The people originally from Crete and ancestors of the Palestinians today.
Peripteros	(Peripteral) A style of pagan temple surrounded by a row of columns on all sides.
Peristyle courtyard	An inner court surrounded with columns.
Pithos	(Pl. pithoi) Large baked clay jar.
Polygonal masonry	A way of constructing walls by fitting polygonal shaped stones together.
Pronaos	The section of ancient Greek temple between the antae and befor the cella.
Propylon	(Plural: porpylaia) Monumental gateway providing access to a temenos.
Prostylos	(Prostyle) A style of pagan temple with columns along the façade and between the antae.
Quadriga	A chariot drawn by four horses.

Ridge beam	The beam forming the top of a roof.
Stele	A monument of a single block of stone.
Stylobate	In ancient achitecture, the upper foundation on which the building and the columns stood.
Synthronon	The steps in the apse of a church, where the clergy sat.
Temenos	A holy area containing one or more temples and surrounded by a wall called peribolos.
Tessera	The small cubes used to make mosaic.
Tetrarchy	Roman government structure where power is shared by four people.
Torso	A human statue with missing arms, legs and head.
Vomitorium	In Roman theatres, the vaulted passageways under the rows of seats for the entrance and exit of the spectators.

SELECTED BIBLIOGRAPHY

Both sites have been introduced in a general sense in: Xanthos, Dossiers de l'Archéologie, 239, décembre 1998.

Abbreviations

AnatAnt : Anatolia Antiqua, Istanbul-Paris

CRAI   : Comptes-Rendus de l'Académie des Inscriptions et Belles-Lettres, Paris

FdeX   : Fouilles de Xanthos, Paris

R.A.   : Revue Archéologique, Paris

DOP   : Dumbarton Oaks Papers, WaDC

Scientific Publications

Fouilles de Xanthos (Paris) Series :

I P. Demargne, Les piliers funéraires, 1958

II H.Metzger, L'acropole lycienne, 1963

III P.Demargne et P.Coupel, Le Monument des Néréides, I, L'architecture, 1969

IV H. Metzger, Les céramiques archaïques et classiques de l'acropole lycienne, 1972

V P. Demargne, Tombes maisons, tombes rupestres et sarcophages, 1974

VI H. Metzger, E. Laroche, A. Dupont-Sommer, M. Mayrhoffer, La stèle trilingue du Létoon, 1979

VII A. Balland, Inscriptions d'époque impériale du Létoon, 1981

VIII P. Demargne et W.A.P. Childs, Le Monument des Néréides, II, Le décor sculpté, 1989

IX H. Metzger, J. Marcadé, G. Siebert, J. Bousquet, A. Davesne, La région Nord du sanctuaire et les inscriptions gréco-lyciennes, 1992

Recent Articles

Chr. Le Roy, "Xanthos-Létoon" in, K.Sams (ed.), Encyclopedia of Anatolian Archaeology içinde

J. des Courtils, "Nouvelles données sur le rempart de Xanthos", REA 96 (1994), 285-298

J. des Courtils, "Un nouveau bas-relief archaïque de Xanthos", RA, 1995, 337-364

Ph. Gauthier, "Bienfaiteurs du gymnase au Létôon de Xanthos", REG 109 (1996), 1-34

M.-P. Raynaud, "La composition en croix de U dans la mosaïque de pavement", RA, 1996, 69-102

J. des Courtils, T. Marksteiner, "Un établissement fortifié dans le voisinage de Xanthos", Anat.Ant. 5 (1997), 87-100

Xanthos, Dossiers d'Archéologie, n°239, décembre 1998

J. Burdy, P. Lebouteiller, "L'aqueduc romain de Xanthos", Anat.Ant., 6 (1998), p. 227-248

D. Laroche et J.-F. Bernard, "Un projet pour l'aménagement des sites de Xanthos et du Létôon", Anat.Ant., 6 (1998), p. 479-490

J. des Courtils, T. Marksteiner, "Long Mur au Nord de Xanthos", Anat.Ant., 7 (1999), p. 89-104.

J. des Courtils, T. et B. Marksteiner, "Un nouveau site lycien près de Xanthos", Anat.Ant., 8 (2000), p. 143-158.

L. Cavalier, "Deux empereurs romains à Xanthos", Anat.Ant., 9 (2001), p. 101-104

Recent Excavation Reports

Since 1997: Anatolia Antiqua (De Boccard Edition-Diffusion, 11, rue de Médicis, 75006 Paris) periodical.

For more bibliographical information see:
www.ausonius.montaigne.u-bordeaux.fr/progr.html

ILLUSTRATIONS

Photographs

All photographs and drawings belong to the French Archaeological Mission.

Plans

Apart from the map by P. Lebouteiller showing Xanthos and environs, all others have been prepared by J.-F. Bernard (French Anatolian Studies Institute).

ALSO AVAILABLE

PRIENE, A Guide to the "Pompeii of Asia Minor"
Frank Rumscheid (1998)

PRIENE Rehberi "Küçük Asya'nın Pompeisi"
Frank Rumscheid (1998)

PRIENE, Führer Durch das "Pompeji Kleinasiens"
Frank Rumscheid (1998)

HATTUSHA Guide "A Day in the Hittite Capital"
Jürgen Seeher (2. Ed, 2002)

HATTUŞA Rehberi "Hitit Başkentinde Bir Gün"
Jürgen Seeher (2. Baskı, 2002)

HATTUSCHA Führer "Ein Tag in der Hethitischen Hauptstadt"
Jürgen Seeher (2. Ed., 2002)

EPHESUS "The New Guide"
Austrian Archaeological Institute (2000)

EFES "Yeni Rehber"
Avusturya Arkeoloji Enstitüsü (2000)

Guide to TROİA
M. Korfmann (3. Ed., 2001)

TROİA Rehberi
M. Korfmann (3. Baskı, 2001)

Führer durch TROİA
M. Korfmann (3. Ed., 2001)

HIERAPOLIS OF PHRYGIA (PAMUKKALE)
"An Archaeological Guide", Francesco D'Andria (2003)

HİERAPOLİS - PAMUKKALE
"Arkeoloji Rehberi", Francesco D'Andria (2003)

HIERAPOLIS DI FRIGIA (PAMUKKALE)
"Guida Archeologica", Francesco D'Andria (2003)

HIERAPOLIS IN PHRYGIEN (PAMUKKALE)
"Ein Archäologischer Führer", Francesco D'Andria (2003)

KLAROS "Apollon Klarios Bilicilik Merkezi"
Nuran Şahin (1998)

Converted Byzantine Churches in Istanbul
"Their Transformation into Mosques and Masjids"
Süleyman Kırımtayıf (2. Ed. 2003)

SİNAN, An Interpretation
Hans G. Egli (1997)

TARABYA, Geschichte und Entwicklung der historischen
Sommerresidenz des deutschen Botschafters am Bosporus
Martin Bachmann (2003)

TARABYA, Alman Büyükelçisi'nin
Boğaziçi'ndeki tarihi yazlık rezidansının tarihçesi ve gelişimi
Martin Bachmann (2003)

FROM KROISOS TO KARIA
Early Anatolian Coins from the Muharrem Kayhan Collection
Koray Konuk (2003)

KARUN'DAN KARİA'YA
Muharrem Kayhan Koleksiyonundan Erken Anadolu Sikkeleri
Koray Konuk (2003)

Distribution

Ege Yayınları
Aslan Yatağı Sokak, Sedef Palas Apt. No.35/2 Cihangir
34433 Istanbul - Turkey
Tel: +90 (212) 249 0520 - 244 7521   Fax: +90 (212) 244 3209
e.mail: zero@kablonet.com.tr